TEACHING EFL WRITING – A PRACTICAL APPROACH FOR SKILLS-INTEGRATED CONTEXTS

Dados Internacionais de Catalogação na Publicação (CIP)

V726t Villas Boas, Isabela de Freitas.
Teaching EFL writing : a practical approach for skills : integrated contexts / Isabela de Freitas Villas Boas. — São Paulo, SP : Cengage Learning, 2017.
136 p. : il. ; 23 cm.

Inclui bibliografia.
ISBN 978-85-221-2780-1

1. Língua inglesa - Estudo e ensino. 2. Escrita. I. Título.

CDU 802.0
CDD 428

Índice para catálogo sistemático:
1. Língua inglesa : Estudo e ensino 802.0

(Bibliotecária responsável: Sabrina Leal Araujo — CRB 10/1507)

TEACHING EFL WRITING – A PRACTICAL APPROACH FOR SKILLS-INTEGRATED CONTEXTS

ISABELA DE FREITAS VILLAS BOAS

Austrália • Brasil • México • Cingapura • Reino Unido • Estados Unidos

Teaching EFL writing – A practical approach for skills-integrated contexts
Isabela de Freitas Villas Boas

Editorial manager: Noelma Brocanelli
Development editor: Salete Del Guerra
Acquisitions editor: Guacira Simonelli
Graphic production: Fabiana Alencar Albuquerque
Rights Specialist: Jenis Oh
Appendixes developed by Angela Minella (A) and Ana Netto (B)
Proofreader: Katy Cox, Raquel Strachicini
Internal designer: Crayon Editorial
Cover designer: Alberto Mateus

© 2018 Cengage Learning Edições Ltda.

All rights reserved. No part of this work covered by the copyright herein may be reproduced, transmitted, stored, or used in any form or by any means graphicgraphic, electronic, or mechanical, including but not limited to photocopying, recording, scanning, digitizing, taping, Web distribution, information networks, or information storage and retrieval systems. According to: Law 9.610/98.

> For product information assistance, contact us at
> **0800 11 19 39**
> Further permissions questions can be emailed to
> **direitosautorais@cengage.com**

© 2018 Cengage Learning. All Rights Reserved.

ISBN 13: 978-85-221-2780-1
ISBN 10: 85-221-2780-8

Cengage Learning
Condomínio E-Business Park
Rua Werner Siemens, 111 – Prédio 11 – Torre A – Conjunto 12
Lapa de Baixo – CEP 05069-900 – São Paulo – SP
Tel.: (11) 3665-9900 Fax: 3665-9901
SAC: 0800 11 19 39

For your course and learning solutions, visit
www.cengage.com.br

Impresso no Brasil
Printed in Brazil
1ª impressão 2017

Acknowledgements

This book is the result of almost twenty years of research and practice in the field of second language writing in an EFL context. I developed an interest in writing early on in my school life because of the positive feedback I received on my writing both in Portuguese as a first language and English as a second language. My confidence in writing and my recognized skills led me to pursue a degree in journalism. However, I began teaching English while in college and developed a passion for the profession, which resulted in my decision to specialize in the field and pursue a Master's Degree in Teaching English as a Second Language from Arizona State University. My applied project was about portfolio assessment of EFL writing. Upon my return to Brazil, I implemented innovations in the teaching of writing at Casa Thomas Jefferson, Brasilia, such as the use of scoring rubrics, portfolio assessment in writing courses, and peer revision. My doctorate in Education was also in the field of literacy and my thesis examined the convergences and divergences between the process-based approach adopted in an English Language Teaching Institute and the product one emphasized in K-12 schools in Brasilia at the time. The major innovation I implemented after my doctorate studies was the adoption of a genre-based approach to teaching writing at Casa Thomas Jefferson, alongside the already adopted process approach.

As my trajectory above depicts, I would not be writing about writing had it not been for all the Portuguese and ESL/EFL* teachers I've had, who

---

* English as a Second Language and English as a Foreign Language.

have helped me develop as a confident writer and provided effective and constructive feedback.

In addition, the practical application of my studies and research would not have been possible without the support of my Casa Thomas Jefferson colleagues, who have trusted and believed in the changes I have proposed in these past twenty years. I would particularly like to thank all past and current course supervisors with whom I have worked on the development of a writing curriculum. I would also like to thank the Executive Director, Lucia Santos, for her trust and support, and above all, my mentor, Katy Cox, who has helped me become a better writer by reviewing my work throughout all these years and providing invaluable orientation and feedback.

Table of contents

CHAPTER 1 › Why focus on writing in the EFL classroom   1
Why teachers avoid talking about writing 4
Why teachers should talk more about writing 7

CHAPTER 2 › The teaching of writing – then and now   11
The product and current-traditional rhetoric approaches . . . 12
The process approach 13
The "post-process" framework and the genre approach . . . 16
The process-genre framework 17

CHAPTER 3 › Stages of the writing process: genre analysis   23
Types of genres 26
Choosing the genres to focus on 27
Analyzing genres and manipulating models 29
Beyond analysis – explicit instruction 35

CHAPTER 4 › Generating ideas and planning   39
Generating Ideas 40
Planning 43
Conclusion 49

CHAPTER 5 › Peer feedback   51
How to make peer feedback work 53
Examples of peer feedback activities 59
Peer feedback in earlier stages of the writing process . . . 65

CHAPTER 6 › **Teacher feedback**   69
Practical guidelines for effective teacher feedback 71
Conferencing 76
Using technology for feedback 77
Teaching students to become independent editors 79

CHAPTER 7 › **Assessing student writing**   83
Scoring rubrics 85
Examples of analytic scales 89
Portfolio assessment 94
Timed compositions and compositions on tests 99

CHAPTER 8 › **Putting it all together: using the process-genre framework to adapt materials**   103

APPENDIX A › **Writing assignment to accompany an intermediate-level (B1) course book** 109

APPENDIX B › **Writing assignment to accompany an advanced-level (C1) course book** 115

References 123

Chapter 1

Why focus on writing in the EFL classroom

Before your read

- Think about your experience learning English-as-a-foreign-language if you are a non-native teacher, or learning another foreign language if you are a native teacher. How much emphasis was placed on writing in your course?
- How much training in the teaching of second language writing have you received so far? Do you think it has been enough to fully equip you to teach second language writing?
- Do you think writing is a topic that is usually addressed in the conferences you attend? Why or why not? When it is, do you tend to go to talks and workshops on the topic of writing?

The field of teaching English as a second or foreign language is relatively new and, thus, historically, it has drawn from studies, theories and approaches in the fields of linguistics, education, and psychology. When it comes to second language (L2) writing[1], before the 1970's, it was either seen as a mere support to the teaching of grammar and vocabulary, or its pedagogy was based on theories and approaches to teaching first language writing, coming out of English or Composition and Rhetoric departments, and L2 teachers had to adapt the approaches to teaching first language writing to their second language context. As the field of second language writing grew and researchers began to learn more about the process of composing in a second or foreign language, new approaches and methods were developed.

Second language writing is now a field in itself, with a prominent journal dedicated solely to research in the field, the *Journal of Second Language Writing*, and a large research community in the United States, the United Kingdom, Australia, New Zealand, and around the world. All authoritative English-language-teaching (ELT) methodology books have a chapter on teaching writing, and there are a number of well-known books dedicated to this topic (FERRIS and HEDGCOCK, 2005; HARMER, 2004; HYLAND, 2003; KASTEN, 2010; MATSUDA et al., 2006; NATION, 2009). Hence, considering the vast literature and research on the topic of second language writing, one could possibly conclude that writing has the same status as the other four skills – speaking, listening and reading - and the subskills of grammar and vocabulary. It is true that in intensive English programs in American universities, for example, writing does have the same status as the other skills, as the classes are usually divided into the four skills, or listening and speaking are grouped together, as well as reading and writing. This applies to many English-as-a-foreign-language (EFL) higher education contexts around the world as well. Likewise, in primary and secondary English-as-a-second language (ESL) contexts, the teaching of writing is also highly emphasized, as students need to master this skill to be successful in their school assignments. English-for-specific

---

[1] Even though the focus of this book is on writing in an English-as-a-foreign-language context, the term second language writing is going to be used because it now constitutes a field in its own right, as opposed to first language writing.

purposes (ESP) classes both in second language and foreign language contexts will also tend to place a balanced focus on writing, especially in areas such as Business English, Legal English and other professional fields. In courses dedicated exclusively to writing, or to the integration of reading and writing, teachers are more likely to have specific training in the teaching of L2 writing, and there are numerous writing or reading and writing course books that follow contemporary approaches, as will be presented in Chapter 2.

However, this is not true in all contexts. In countries where English is not the native language and, thus, students attending English courses may or may not need to write proficiently in English in their current daily lives, the focus on writing can vary significantly, as it can be taught as a mere back-up to the teaching of other skills – writing for learning - or it can be taught as a skill in its own right – writing for writing (HARMER, 2004). For example, when students complete written exercises focused on grammar and vocabulary, when they answer questions about the texts that they have read or listened to, when they take notes on grammar explanations and vocabulary definitions and examples, or when they write dialogues to present to the class, writing is used to practice another skill or subskill, not as a skill in its own right.

Conversely, when students produce texts in specific genres for a specific communicative purpose, then they are engaged in writing for writing. This difference is not so clear-cut, though. Suppose a teacher asks students to write a paragraph about their last weekend, with a view to verifying whether students are using the simple past of regular and irregular verbs correctly. This might seem at first glance to be a writing activity in itself. Nevertheless, if the focus is merely on practicing grammar, then it is only writing for learning. There is nothing misguided in assigning writing for learning activities. In fact, integration of skills is highly recommended in the contemporary language classroom, and writing should be integrated with speaking, listening, and reading. More than that, grammar should be presented and practiced in discourse, that is, beyond the sentence, so it makes sense to ask students to write paragraphs to demonstrate their knowledge of grammar. However, If language programs want students to develop their communicative competence to its fullest extent, and to use English proficiently to achieve different social, academic, and professional goals, then they also need to save time in their curriculum for writing for writing.

Skills-integrated course books by well-known international publishers also vary significantly in the emphasis placed on writing. Some may include writing activities in every unit, while others will focus on writing in every other unit or perhaps only in the workbook assignments. Some course books only present a writing prompt, usually linked to the topic of the lesson and to the input students have received in listening and reading, while others offer some sort of writing curriculum in which different rhetorical skills are focused on in each unit. However, very few of them contain a solid writing curriculum, focused on a variety of genres, and with writing activities that address all the different stages of the writing process. Unlike the teachers in writing classes, teachers in skills-integrated programs do not necessarily have specific training in the teaching of L2 writing. They are language teachers, not writing teachers. Thus, they will tend to do only what the course book proposes, as they have little idea how they can complement their course books in order to fully focus on the development of their students' writing skills.

Why teachers avoid talking about writing

Writing is not a hot topic among teachers. One can conclude this when going to ELT conferences. How many talks and workshops are there about teaching second language writing as compared to other topics? Writing is usually underrepresented in the local, national, and international conferences I attend. Why is this so? Why don't teachers like to talk about writing? Here are some reasons commonly mentioned, followed by some arguments against them:

1   Teachers don't give due importance to writing because they themselves don't write much.

It is true that not only teachers, but people in general, write very little these days. Besides lesson plans, reports on students' performance, a few professional and personal e-mails, and social media posts now and then, how much else do teachers have to write on a daily basis? And if they don't have to write much, they also think their students won't have to write much either. However, it is the ability to express ideas clearly in writing and catch the readers' attention that has led many teachers to advance in their careers and become well-known in their professional learning communities by way of blogs and conference presentations. In order to be accepted as a presenter in a major conference, one has to be able to write an effective presentation proposal, with coherence, cohesion, and correct use of language. In addition, all teacher development certificates and degrees require a great amount of writing from teachers. In all these cases, writing can be either a barrier or an advantage, depending on the teacher's writing skills. Thus, teachers who want to continue advancing in their career should consider it important to write in the language that they teach and should make it a point to continue developing as writers.

2   It's very difficult to teach writing in the EFL classroom because students don't like it and don't see a purpose in it.

Indeed, writing is a difficult skill to teach because it is culturally-acquired, rather than species-specific, and there is great variability in the extent to which it is fully acquired (BROWN, 1994). However, if it is difficult to teach writing, shouldn't it be the other way around, that is, because it is a difficult skill to teach, shouldn't there be more people presenting on writing and more people attending these presentations? Why do we avoid talking about writing? We also need to consider the root of the problem: the main reason why students don't like writing is because they find the task daunting. They don't know what to write and how to do it. It doesn't have to be like this, though. A well-planned writing lesson, with a focus on all the stages of the writing process and explicit teaching of the rhetorical and linguistic features of the genre students will have to write, will certainly make writing more palatable to students. When they feel confident about what to write and how to do it, students begin to see writing differently and to value it, especially if the tasks are based on their current and future real-life needs and this is explicitly shown to them. Not learning more about writing because students don't like it leads teachers to teach writing ineffectively, which leads students to dislike writing and also to write ineffectively, creating a vicious cycle.

3. Students (especially teenagers) don't have to do much writing in EFL anyway, so why give much emphasis to it in the skills-integrated classroom?

We hear again and again that nowadays teens and young adults don't write anymore; they only do texting or voice/video recording. This might be true for some teens and young adults, but how about bloggers and vloggers? The former certainly have to write and so do the latter, as they probably write scripts or at least outlines of what they will record. The ability to organize ideas both in writing and in speaking and to engage their audience is what makes these social influencers succeed. Isn't this what students learn when they write? Besides, when we are learning a language at a younger age, we don't know yet the purposes for which we will have to use that language in the future. However, we need to acquire the necessary skills to use the language in a variety of formal and informal settings, for personal, professional and academic purposes. A teenager is not learning English only to be able to use English as a teenager. In a few years, they might have to write college and/or job applications, statements of purpose, formal e-mails and a whole host of other genres. Even adults who are learning English only for personal reasons, for travel and leisure, might find themselves in the future writing an e-mail of complaint or a hotel or restaurant review. Just as it can be for teachers, writing is a gatekeeper in many professions. Those who can write well in English have a great advantage.

4. Writing can only be taught fully and effectively in a writing course or in an exam-prep course, not in a "regular" EFL course. Thus, writing teachers and exam-prep teachers are the ones who should be talking about writing.

Perhaps many programs use writing as a back-up for grammar teaching and do not focus on writing for writing, only on writing for learning. The fact that most course books give little emphasis to writing and rarely present complete writing lessons, with all the stages of the writing process, especially planning and generating ideas and a focus on different genres, is probably proof that this is not what most programs want. However, it is possible to teach writing as a skill in its own right in a skills-integrated program and make it meaningful to students. The types of writing addressed in exams do not encompass the full range of genres that students will have to produce in their real lives. In addition, writing should be practiced in tandem with the other skills.

Why teachers should talk more about writing

In order to argue in favor of a greater emphasis on writing in skills-integrated programs, below are some of the contemporary topics in ELT nowadays and how they relate to the writing skill.

1   Critical thinking

Bloom's revised taxonomy (KRATHWOHL, 2002) has been repeatedly mentioned in the past few years, and it is indeed important that we carry out activities that develop higher order thinking skills, such as analyzing, evaluating, and creating. Writing plays an integral role in these three processes.

When students compose texts in different genres, after having gone through the process of analyzing the given genre, generating ideas and planning their writing, drafting, engaging in self and peer assessment, and rewriting, the highest levels of critical thinking are involved. Thus, a well-developed writing lesson is crucial in every classroom in which developing critical thinking is a goal.

2   Bilingual education

CLIL (Content-language Integrated Learning) is about developing academic literacy, and a major component is writing in the different content areas. Students need to learn to write lab reports, book reviews, essays, summaries, and other types of genres in order to be fully academically literate. Knowing how to implement the genre approach to ESL/EFL writing is, thus, a skill every teacher in a bilingual education context needs to develop.

3   Technology and 21st Century skills

Besides critical thinking, there are other 21st Century skills that need attention in every classroom, such as collaboration, communication, and creativity. Again, well developed writing assignments can easily tap into these skills. Meaningful, authentic topics, written for real-life purposes, can give students a genuine sense of communication. Students can work collaboratively on pieces of writing using Google Docs and other resources, as well as give feedback to each other using technology. They can write scripts that then become videos produced either individually or collaboratively, and they can subsequently provide written feedback on each other's videos. Project-based learning is also supported by writing, as many projects require some sort of written artifact.

4   Assessment

Another topic that has been extensively addressed recently is assessment, with a special focus on formative and authentic assessment. Process writing, which will be addressed in the next chapter, is the quintessential example of formative assessment because it allows students the opportunity to receive feedback from peers and the teacher and revise their writing, ideally as many times as necessary. It is a true example of assessment for learning rather than of learning. Furthermore, by way of writing assignments, one can assess students' language development in a much more authentic manner than with selected-response or fill-in-the-blanks exercises. Performance tasks assess learners' authentic production in either speaking or writing. It is no wonder that the Internet-based TOEFL (TOEFL iBT) assesses grammar use by way of speaking and writing activities, rather than discrete test items.

Summing up, it seems that course books don't include full writing assignments because publishers know that writing is not emphasized in all the markets they want to reach. The reasons why writing is not emphasized may vary, but they probably include beliefs about what the students may or may not want or need and also about teachers' expertise and willingness to teach writing effectively, as we have to admit that reading students' countless papers is an additional burden for teachers. Teachers, in turn, feel insecure teaching writing because they do not find much support in the course books, they probably received little training regarding teaching L2 writing, and so they tend to avoid this topic.

This book is addressed to teachers-in-training or teachers in skills-integrated EFL programs who have no or very little training in the teaching of second language writing, who may write very little in the language they teach, and also perhaps wrote very little in the courses they took while in their teacher education programs, and who might not have experienced, as learners, the second language writing instruction that is purported here. While the most well-known methodology textbooks have a chapter dedicated to teaching writing, it is usually limited to very basic and limited information regarding how to address each stage of the writing process. Conversely, the prominent books on second language writing are too extensive and academic, and most are aimed primarily at teachers of writing per se, not necessarily teachers who teach writing along with other skills and will probably not read a 200-plus-page book addressing the theory and practice of second language writing. The purpose of this book, thus, is to provide a practical framework for the teaching of writing in skills-integrated EFL programs that is accessible to any teacher and that will empower teachers to select the right materials, adapt any materials they use, or even create their own materials in order to teach writing to its full extent in their classrooms.

> **After your read**
>
> - Do you agree with the reasons why teachers don't like to talk about writing? Would you have more reasons to add?
> - Can you think of other reasons why writing should be more emphasized than it is in skills-integrated EFL contexts?
> - What do you expect to learn about second language writing in this book?

Chapter 2
The teaching of writing – then and now

> **Before your read**
>
> - Think about a typical writing lesson in your L1, perhaps when you were in high school or college. What was the lesson like? How did you receive feedback on your writing? What kinds of texts did you produce? Was the focus on the language, on the type of text, or on writing strategies?
> - Now think about a typical writing lesson in your L2 and answer the same questions as above.
> - How similar is the way you teach L2 writing to the way you learned L1 and L2 writing?

Though the purpose of this book is not to overwhelm teachers with extensive information on the history of L2 writing or research, it is important to provide EFL teachers with a brief overview of the approaches that have been prevalent throughout history, some of which still coexist around the world. This way, teachers will be better equipped to make informed decisions about the materials they use and how they can be supplemented according to the practical framework that will be provided from Chapter 3 on.

The product and current-traditional rhetoric approaches

Before the mid-1960's, the teaching of writing in L1 was reduced to correcting papers (KROLL, 1991), in what is now called the product approach, since the teaching of writing strategies was of no concern. Students received topics to write about and had their papers marked by the teacher. Meanwhile, the dominant L2 teaching method was the Audio-lingual Method, in which writing was considered secondary, as "language" was speech. Learning to write in a second language was an exercise in habit formation and there was no concern regarding audience and purpose (SILVA, 1990). The writing task was very controlled to prevent learners from making mistakes. Typical writing tasks at that time consisted of transforming a narrative in the present tense to the past tense, for example, or reproducing in writing a text read by the teacher (dictogloss). Writing was a secondary skill and used for learning grammar and vocabulary; that is, there was writing for learning, but not writing for writing.

A few years later, controlled composition proved to be ineffective in improving students' ability to produce extended discourse, and an approach to L1 writing called current-traditional rhetoric was adapted in ESL teaching, combined with Kaplan's theory of contrastive rhetoric (SILVA, 1990), which showed how different languages also had different rhetorical features. Because the first language was found to interfere beyond the sentence level, the focus was shifted from linguistic to rhetorical form and writing began to be taught as a skill, but with a focus solely on the final product. Attention was given to the paragraph and its components (topic sentence, supporting sentences, and concluding sentences). These paragraph principles were extrapolated to larger stretches of discourse and emphasis was given to structure (introduction, development, and conclusion) and organizational patterns (narration, description, exposition, and argumentation). Essays were written in one draft and the teacher's feedback focused on syntactic and rhetorical form. Students practiced writing topic sentences and outlining their five-paragraph essays, the primary genre that was taught in the L2 classroom, as it was the genre demanded in the well-known standardized proficiency tests at the time.

The process approach

In the late 1960's, there was a shift in L1 composition teaching from a focus on product to a focus on process, a consequence of various studies demonstrating that the ways student-writers produce text do not necessarily match the model that had been traditionally promulgated. It took some time for these insights from L1 pedagogy to be integrated into L2 teaching (KROLL, 1991). Dissatisfaction with both the controlled composition and the current-traditional approach motivated the introduction of the process approach in ESL composition teaching. It was felt that expression of thought was neglected in both of these approaches, which were prescriptive and treated composing a linear process. Zamel (1983, p. 165), on the contrary, describes composing as a "non-linear, exploratory, and generative process whereby writers discover and reformulate their ideas as they attempt to approximate meaning". Grabe and Kaplan (1996) also relate the dissatisfaction with conventional approaches to the increased number of minority students in the US tertiary institutions. It was found that students with vastly different life experiences did not benefit from an approach that was acceptable in an educational system designed for the culturally homogeneous elite and middle class.

The Process Approach attributes a significant role to the writer and the process through which he/she creates and produces discourse (JOHNS, 1990). Organizational patterns or syntactic constraints are not imposed upon the writer. Form is determined by content, ideas, and the need to communicate.

Classroom tasks are characterized by the use of journals, invention, peer collaboration, revision, and attention to content before form (RAIMES, 1991). Students are allowed time for selecting topics, generating ideas, and writing drafts and revisions. There are other important features of the process approach: self-discovery and authorial voice; meaningful writing on topics of importance or interest to the writer; the need to plan out writing as a goal-oriented, contextualized activity; and students' awareness of the writing process and of notions such as audience, voice, plans, etc. (GRABE and KAPLAN, 1996).

The Process Approach has gone through four major stages since its creation, each one with its own emphasis. The expressive stage originated in the 1960's and placed emphasis on the writer, who should look for authentic voices, express themselves freely, and take chances. Proponents of this version view writing as a vehicle for self-revelation and self-discovery; students are given assignments that require them to reflect on and analyze their own personal experiences. It was believed that the writing skills learned in producing personal writing would transfer to the skills required to produce academic papers (KROLL, 1991, p. 255).

Research in cognitive psychology led to the emergence of the cognitive approach to the writing process, in which writing is seen as a problem-solving task. Emphasis is given on planning: defining the rhetorical problem, placing it in a larger context, making it operational, exploring its parts, generating alternative solutions, and arriving at well-supported conclusions. The writing process continues after the planning stage, when students transfer their thoughts into words, revise, and edit (JOHNS, 1990). Developing students' metacognitive awareness of the writing process is a priority in this approach, and great emphasis is placed on responses to writing (HYLAND, 2003).

In the 1980's, a new group of researchers began adopting a sociolinguistic perspective that saw writing as dependent upon the social context which defines its purpose. Writing is not the product of a single individual; it echoes the voices of the discourse community. Within this framework, there are two possible points of focus, namely, the content or the reader. A focus on the content involves teaching the learner the rhetorical conventions of their specific academic field, whereas a focus on the reader implies that writing is influenced by the values, expectations, and conventions of the discourse communities that will consume the text. Students should thus be familiarized with the thinking styles and discourse that are typical of their academic community so that they can be active participants in such a community (CANAGARAJAH, 2002).

What is important to consider is that these four approaches to process writing do not have to be mutually exclusive and can be used for different purposes, ages, and levels of students. Beginners, for example, will probably write more personal texts at the paragraph level or other simple, everyday genres, as they still do not have command of transactional vocabulary. As they reach the intermediate level, students will probably begin writing longer paragraphs and practice writing topic sentences, supporting details and conclusions, so they can develop writing strategies. Upper intermediate and advanced students need to produce texts for clear social purposes, to reach a specific discourse community. There is room in the EFL classroom for writing as a personal, cognitive, and social activity.

Regardless of the version of the process approach, Grabe (2001) summarizes the elements that ESL writing pedagogy should generally include: a) extensive practice; b) long-term curricular planning with a view to developing writing abilities; c) consistent exposition to a wide variety of texts and tasks; d) opportunities for appropriate feedback and revision; e) opportunities to discuss textual production and its revision vis-à-vis the proposed objectives; f) models of texts that present reasonable solutions to the tasks proposed; g) tasks that motivate the students. The notion of process is clearly present in these premises.

Boscolo (2008) suggests using the term "process approaches" in the plural, since there have been many variations of the approach. In its original and "strong" version, the process approach has the following characteristics:

a   Expository classes are minimized and group work is emphasized;
b   Students should be allowed to choose the topics to write about;

c   The teacher is not a judge, but rather, a facilitator who provides feedback to students in individual conferences;

d   The social dimension of writing is emphasized, for students work in groups and read each other's writings.

The "post-process" framework and the genre approach

In the beginning of the third millennium, the teaching of writing has reached a more balanced perspective in which writing is viewed not only as a means of self-expression or as a problem-solving activity, but as a social act of communication. There's a balance between process and product, and the classroom is a community with students as active participants in the construction of their writing and of that of their colleagues. In addition, the close interrelationship between reader and writer is acknowledged (REID, 2001).

Atkinson (2003) calls this the post-process era, in which there has been a socio-cultural turn. However, rather than a paradigm shift, the post-process approach is an expansion and broadening of the domain of L2 writing. Hence, it does not preclude using a process approach to writing, and pre-writing, drafting, feedback, and revising are still regarded effective classroom activities.

Genre-based pedagogy came to expand the notion of L2 writing as going beyond the planning-writing-reviewing framework by focusing on the linguistic resources writers need to communicate effectively, rather than merely on writing strategies (HYLAND, 2007, p. 150). Genres are "abstract, socially recognized ways for using languages for particular purposes" (HYLAND, 2003, p. 18). Writers need to follow certain writing conventions so their readers can recognize their purpose. A set of texts that serve the same purpose often share the same structure and thus belong to the same genre. If students are led to recognize these text structures that are particular of specific genres, they will be able to write effectively in these genres and achieve their communicative goal.

Hyland (2007) argues that genre pedagogies pull together language, content, and context and present students with systematic explanations of how texts exercise their communicative function. Teachers set out the stages, or moves, of valued genres, providing an explicit grammar of linguistic choices within and beyond the sentence (HYLAND, 2003). Genre-based writing instruction follows a method of contextualizing-modeling-negotiating-constructing, in which the teacher has the role of scaffolding the process. Explicit teaching of genres is advocated and students are led to analyze "expert texts" so they can be aware of their linguistic and rhetorical features. After the genre-analysis stage comes the collective construction phase, in which students and teacher construct a text in the genre proposed. Having gone through the joint-construction stage, students are ready to write their own text, redraft and revise it, based on the teacher's feedback. Genre-based pedagogy is particularly useful in a K-12 ESL environment for writing in the content areas (DE OLIVEIRA and LAN, 2014). Nevertheless, its main premises can and should inform EFL writing pedagogy. After all, knowing how to read and produce texts that are considered valuable in second language learners' discourse communities will directly affect how they succeed in their use of the L2 to achieve their social, professional, and academic goals. It is the teachers' job to make these genres of power visible and attainable to students through explicit instruction (HIGHLAND, 2003).

Hyland (2007) justifies a focus on genres in the writing class, enumerates the key features of the genre-based approach, and discusses the characteristics and elements of a writing course focused on genres, from designing the curriculum to choosing the genres and developing a teaching cycle. However, his focus is on academic writing and English-for-Specific-Purposes (ESP) writing courses. Not all his recommendations and premises are applicable in skills-integrated contexts in which writing is not the sole focus, and the teacher does not necessarily design the curriculum or choose the texts or course books to use. However, the genre approach can be adapted to this context and can be followed along with a focus on process writing.

The process-genre framework

As Hyland (2003) contends, while the process and genre orientations may seem incongruent – since the process approach focuses on the cognitive process of composing while the genre approach focuses on the social function of the text – they can actually complement each other: "Writing is a socio-cognitive activity which involves skills in planning and drafting as well as knowledge of language, contexts, and audiences" (HYLAND, 2003, p. 23).

This book proposes a process-genre framework that combines the principles of process writing from the sociocultural perspective and the main elements of the genre approach and that is feasible in skills-integrated EFL classes, adhering to these main premises.

1. The writing process is emphasized, but the final product is also important.
2. Texts of different genres should be used for analysis and as models, with the purpose of linking reading and writing and of raising students' awareness of the linguistic and rhetorical features of different genres.
3. Students should be taught rhetorical patterns and conventions explicitly; we cannot assume that they will pick them up incidentally. Students don't learn to write just by writing. These rhetorical patterns and conventions should be linked to the genre students are producing.
4. Teachers should plan their instruction in order to encompass all the stages of the writing process: generating ideas, planning, drafting, revising, assessing, and giving and receiving feedback. They should also remember that writers don't go about these stages linearly, but rather recursively.
5. Feedback on writing should not be provided only by the teacher and it should provide specific guidelines to the writer about what needs to be improved in the text regarding content, organization, and language use, with a focus on whether the writing has met the audience's expectations, based on the genre and its social purpose.

The learning cycle proposed in this framework mixes the genre-based cycle and the process-based one, comprising the stages presented in Figure 2.1. Depending on the result of student production, the teacher might have to go back to earlier stages for improvement.

The teaching of writing – then and now

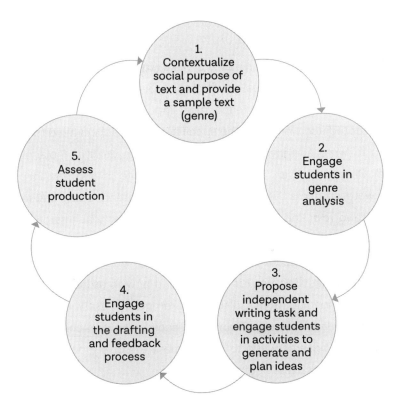

Figure 2.1 - The learning cycle in the process-genre framework

As discussed in the previous chapter, there is a tendency for writing to be downplayed in skills-integrated EFL courses due to the many reasons presented, the main one being teachers' lack of knowledge related to how to actually teach writing effectively in these contexts, leading to two possible reactions: 1) Do what is in the course book; 2) Do not work with writing because there is no time to engage students in all the stages of the writing process and focus on the other skills and subskills that the curriculum encompasses. In fact, reading about the history of L2 writing instruction and the premises underlying the process-genre framework, one might wonder whether all this can be accomplished outside the writing classroom. The answer is yes, and the following chapters will focus explicitly on how to address the distinct stages of a writing assignment with realistic expectations from students within the constraints of a skills-integrated context and all the other types of assignments students might have to carry out.

The first decision teachers have to make regards the genre their students will tackle. Chapter 3 focuses on different types of genres, how to choose them, and how to explicitly teach their linguistic and rhetorical features. Having selected and worked on the specific genre, teachers need to motivate students to write and involve them in generating ideas and planning, the focus of Chapter 4. With a specific genre to write in and having planned what to write, students then need to engage in drafting, giving and receiving feedback, and rewriting. Chapter 5 will focus on how teachers can engage students in the feedback-giving process, while Chapter 6 addresses how they, teachers, should give feedback on their students' writing, with practical and authentic examples. Chapter 7 is dedicated to how to assess writing by way of assignment-specific rubrics, also with examples to use with different age and proficiency levels. Finally, Chapter 8 discusses how teachers can use the knowledge they have acquired to complement the often-incomplete writing assignments in the course books they use.

After your read

- How much of the information presented in this chapter were you already familiar with and how much was new to you?
- Have you ever experienced the process and the genre approaches as a student? Have you ever used them as a teacher?
- Among the topics of the subsequent chapters, which ones are you least familiar with?

TEACHERS WILL BE BETTER EQUIPPED

Chapter 3

Stages of the writing process: genre analysis

Before your read

- Think about what you have written in your native language lately (if you are a non-native teacher). What was the purpose of your writing? Can you identify the genres you used?
- What about in English? What did you write? For what purpose? What are the most common genres you write in in English?
- What are the usual genres you have your students write in English and how to you decide?

As Hyland (2003) argues, writing is not only a personal and individual activity, but also an interactional and social one which reflects the writer's engagement in a particular discourse community. Learning how to write in a second language cannot be reduced to mastering a set of technical abilities or simply having opportunities to write and receive feedback from peers and from the teacher. It also involves knowledge of the ways the target discourse communities communicate, the genres they use to frame their social action, that is, to act in society. Genres are "self-reinforcing, recognizable forms of communication" (BAZERMAN, 2004, p. 316).

Below are the beginnings of different pieces of writing, written in different genres. How easy is it for you to recognize these genres?

Once upon time ...
TO WHOM IT MAY CONCERN
The purpose of this ... is to ...
First, pour
A fifteen-year old male was arrested last night while he was ...
Love, ...
BTW, plz ... LOL
It was found that, among the subjects studied, 89% ...

Figure 3.1 – Guessing the genre

Our students may be familiar with the genres that are used in their L1 discourse communities, but these may differ from the ones they will need to master for communication in the L2. A genre-based approach to teaching writing does not take for granted that the students will naturally acquire knowledge of how these genres are structured, but rather, that they need explicit instruction in how to produce the genres that will be important for them in their L2 written communication. Writing instruction in the EFL classroom cannot focus only on writing to learn, but also on writing to achieve the many goals our students will need to fulfill in their interactions with their new L2 discourse communities.

The traditional writing assignment in the skills-integrated EFL classroom is the five-paragraph essay. In beginning levels, the assignments focus on writing paragraphs and their components, such as the topic sentence, the supporting details, and the conclusion. Students practice writing narrative, descriptive, expository and persuasive paragraphs. In the intermediate level, students transition from writing paragraphs to writing different types of essays, such as expository, persuasive, process analysis, and comparison and contrast. One of the reasons this is so is due to the predominance of this type of essay in proficiency exams.

This is the washback effect of these exams on the teaching of EFL. Washback refers to the impact that an exam has on teaching. For example, a grammar-based exam can have a negative washback effect on teaching in that teachers who are accountable for the students' success in such exam will focus more on grammar than on the other components of communicative competence. In the case of writing, a focus on the five-paragraph essay in proficiency exams will lead to a greater focus on the five-paragraph essay in the classroom. However, we need to take into consideration that the five-paragraph essay is a school-based type of essay and only one of the many genres that our students need to learn to produce. After all, passing a proficiency exam is only one of the many goals our students have for learning EFL.

There is also a bias especially in more advanced materials towards academic writing. Academic writing is a now a robust field of study and there are many studies and course books focused only on this genre. This is so because most of the second language writing specialists are involved with higher education and teach academic writing. This body of knowledge produced in the second language writing circles many times informs the course books we use. However, writing for an academic audience is one of the purposes of writing that our students will need to master. In a general-English, integrated-skills classroom, we will most probably find students with different goals for learning English, so our choice of genres to focus on needs to address these different goals and needs, and not focus only on academic writing or the five-paragraph essay.

Types of genres

As previously discussed, genres are "abstract, socially-recognized ways of using language for particular purposes" (HYLAND, 2003, p. 21). They are ways of getting something done. We use genres to tell stories, file a complaint, apply for a job, describe a technical process, among many other purposes. Below is a list of written genres compiled from Hyland (2003, p. 19) and expanded.

letter	menu	report	manual	jingle
inventory	joke	sermon	editorial	will
essay	advertisement	lecture	poem	sign
notice	manifesto	label	chat	statement of purpose
warrant	biography	note	song	novel
article	movie review	consultation	blog post	digital presentation
poster	book review	e-mail	infographic	video/movie script
petition	memo	story	list	recipe

Figure 3.2 – List of genres

Source: Adapted from Hyland (2003, p. 19).

These are only some common, more general examples. Letters, for instance, can be of different genres and follow very different patterns, such as personal letters, business letters, letters of recommendation, application letters, letters of complaints, letters to the editor, among others. Reports can also vary in their structure depending on their purpose. For example, an accident report will have a very different text structure from a book report, which, in its turn, will also be very different from a lab report.

The genres exemplified above also differ in their length and level of formality, or register. A jingle, for instance, will use much more informal language than a statement of purpose. A chat will also be more informal than an e-mail or a letter. However, they are all socially-validated forms of communication, and being familiar with them will help students participate in their necessary social interactions.

It is also important to underscore that some of the genres exemplified above will be more useful for students to recognize and read than to produce. Our students will not have to produce all these genres in L2, just as they do not produce all of them in their L1. Thus, we need to be very careful to choose the genres to focus on in the writing classroom so as not to waste students' time and energy producing genres that are not relevant to them.

Choosing the genres to focus on

Our goal is to empower teachers to identify if the writing component of the course books they use fulfills this objective of addressing different, meaningful genres, and, if not, to help them supplement the materials with writing activities that will enable students to participate effectively in their discourse communities. In other words, if the teacher or the language program purports to follow a process-genre approach to the teaching of the writing skill, they may need to develop a writing syllabus beyond the one proposed by the course book adopted. If a course book is not adopted, they will need to design this syllabus. In skills-integrated EFL programs, with levels ranging from beginners to advanced, and ages ranging from children to adults, teachers will usually have a prescribed course book to follow.

The first step then is to analyze the writing assignments presented in the course book series and identify what genres students are asked to write. Next, it is important to identify the genres that the students currently need to produce or will need to produce in the future. One way to do this is to develop a short needs analysis questionnaire and administer it to students. If they are adults, they will probably be able to clearly identify the genres they need or will need to produce. Teenagers and children, though, will probably not have this level of awareness, so the teacher might have to predict what these genres are. Besides, teenagers, especially, will be learning to write in genres that they might not need to master at their present moment of study but that they may need to produce in the near future, such as a statement of purpose or a job application.

Harmer (2004) argues that even if we ask students, it is unlikely that we will go beyond a list of the most general purposes for writing. He adds that it is virtually impossible to develop writing tasks that are directly relevant to a group full of adult students, for example, with varying needs, backgrounds and occupations. He suggests that it is best to "concentrate on a repertoire of writing tasks that it is reasonable to assume that most speakers of English may have to take part in at some stage in their English-speaking lives" (HARMER, 2004, p. 40). Similarly, some researchers suggest a core set of general school genres that are thought to be useful for students to learn because they can be combined in a variety of ways. They include narrative, recount, argument, report, and description (HYLAND, 2003). The *Australian Certificate in the Spoken and Written English* ESL curriculum adopts six broad families of text-types that can help identify the kinds of texts needed as input: exchanges, forms, procedures, information texts, story texts, and persuasive texts (HYLAND, 2003, p. 105).

Another aspect to consider when choosing the genres to focus on regards the student's age and proficiency level. In lower levels, it is more realistic to ask students to produce genres that are short and in which simple sentences and more high-frequency vocabulary are used, such as notes, posters, postcards or thank-you letters. Children should produce genres that are meaningful to them, such as cards, invitations, stories, comic strips, or posters. Blog posts, movie and book reviews, and stories are probably motivating to write for teenagers. However, students at this age level also need to develop their ability to write school and professional genres, especially at the intermediate level and above. Even so, the teacher can make these genres more meaningful to them by adapting the task to their reality. For example, in learning how to write a letter of application, a teenager can be asked to respond to a job ad for aids in a summer camp. The purpose – applying for a job – is still fulfilled, but it is a job that a youngster would realistically apply for, not something imaginary and decontextualized. In genre pedagogy, the notion of writing for a purpose, to fulfill a social need, is of paramount importance.

The writing assignments in the course books adopted might not always engage students in the production of a variety of genres that will be useful for them in their personal, professional and academic lives using L2. However, these will probably contain texts in a variety of genres that can serve as a springboard for a supplementary writing assignment. Other times, there might be a variety of genres depicted in the writing assignments, but these do not engage students in the whole genre-based writing cycle. It will be up to the teacher, then, to identify what is lacking in the writing curriculum and supplement it. Most of the times, the stage that is most lacking is the genre analysis one.

Analyzing genres and manipulating models

The first stage in a genre-based writing assignment is modeling. It is when the students will explicitly and collaboratively discuss and analyze text structure, context, and language, with the teacher's intervention. The process of consciousness-raising allows students to analyze and reflect upon how a text is structured at the discourse level, exploring its key lexical, grammatical, and rhetorical features. This enables students to then construct a text in the same genre. In a writing course, students typically analyze and compare several texts of the same genre, and these texts should be relevant and authentic. In a skills-integrated classroom, though, in which writing is one of the four skills focused on and not necessarily the most important, it might not be feasible to spend time analyzing different texts, so one good example of the genre will suffice. If this text is already included in the materials, perhaps in the reading section, it makes the teacher's job even easier. Also, at lower levels, it might also not be possible to only bring authentic texts for analysis, as they may be way beyond students' proficiency level.

  The purpose of genre analysis activities is for students to develop knowledge of the communicative purpose and rhetorical structure of texts as well as knowledge of readers' expectations and beliefs. Thus, students' attention should be directed to the social purpose, the structure, and the linguistic features of the text, such as the types of grammatical structures, linking devices, and vocabulary used. Here are some of the aspects students' attention can be directed to in a genre analysis activity, starting from the whole and moving to the small parts, adapted from Hyland (2003):

- The purpose of the text: who it is written for and why.
- The tone: formal or informal.
- The relationship between the writer and the intended reader.
- The visual layout and how it fits the social purpose of the text.
- The move structure: what each part aims to achieve.
- The use of headings and images.
- The way the text is divided into paragraphs.
- The use of cohesive devices.
- The use of pronoun references.
- The choice of vocabulary.
- The verb tenses used.
- The sentence types used.
- The types of pronouns used, such as whether personal pronouns are used or not and why.

The analysis of the move structure of the text is a key step in a genre approach. A particular genre will follow a series of moves to fulfill the communicative purpose. The moves in a recipe, for example, are the name of the dish, a list of ingredients and amounts, the steps for cooking, and the number of people the dish serves (MILLAR, 2011). Analyzing the move structure allows students to identify the purpose of each part of the text beyond more general terms such as introduction, development, and conclusion.

It is not necessary to focus on all these features in all assignments, but it is important that within a course, students will have gained awareness of all these features in a text, with the ultimate goal of teaching students how to be successful independent writers. When faced with the need to write in an unfamiliar genre, students will have learned how to research texts in the target genre, notice their major features, and be able to reproduce these features in their own, original texts.

Below is an example of a simple task that helps raise students' awareness to how a letter is organized. Genre awareness was not part of the book activities, so the activity was created[2] with the purpose of filling this gap in the course book.

Most letters have five to six parts. Each part gives different information. Read the letter and complete the information below with the words from the box.

| date | signature | address | greeting | message | closing |

1. The _____ shows the place where the person lives.
2. The _____ shows the day, month and year that Tisha wrote the letter.
3. The _____ gives the name of the person Tisha wrote to.
4. The _____ is what Tisha wants to tell that person.
5. The _____ ends the message.
6. The _____ gives Tisha's name (in her handwriting).

Another very important way of developing students' genre awareness is engaging them in the manipulation of models. These types of tasks require students to combine, insert, reorder or delete text segments (HYLAND, 2003). A typical model manipulation task is one in which students receive scrambled parts of the text and have to put it in order. Other types of manipulation tasks are:

» Matching the first part of sentences with their second parts.
» Filling in blanks with missing items, such as linking words.
» Filling in missing parts such as topic sentences, or choosing the best topic sentence among a number of options.
» Crossing out sentences that do not belong to the text.
» Complete unfinished texts.

---

2. Created by Silvia Caldas, Casa Thomas Jefferson, Brasilia, Brazil.

Below is another example[3] of how a writing activity based on a model provided in the course book was adapted to include genre-awareness activities.

■ **LEVEL: Pre-intermediate**

Step 1: Setting the context: Students read a text about an Afghan refugee who was on the cover of National Geographic in 1985 and was searched for 17 years later by the photographer who had taken the picture. He wanted to know where she was and what she was doing. She was again the cover of National Geographic in 2002 and a fund was created by the National Geographic Society to help Afghan girls. The activities include the pre, while, and post reading stages.

Step 2: Students are provided with a model of a proposal asking for help or donations for a charity. The course book provides the model and asks students to write their own proposal.

Step 3: Supplementary activity: Students analyze the proposal and do the following activities:

1. Read the proposal on page 104 and answer the questions.
   a. Where is the school?
   b. Who built the school?
   c. What is the problem?
   d. Which are the two suggestions made?
   e. How does the person end the proposal?

2. Which of the steps below can you identify in the model proposal?
   a. _____ The writer explains what the problem is.
   b. _____ The writer explains how he feels about the problem.
   c. _____ The writer proposes a solution to the problem.
   d. _____ The writer mentions costs that will be involved.
   e. _____ The writer concludes by restating the problem and the outcome of the proposed action.

The genre analysis activity focuses students' attention on both the content and the form of the model. Activity 2 helps raise students' awareness of what is mentioned and what is not mentioned in the proposal, which is very objective and straightforward.

---

[3] Created by Silvia Caldas, Casa Thomas Jefferson, Brasilia, Brazil.

Stages of the writing process: genre analysis

The aim of the genre analysis activities is to help students identify what information is essential for the proposal and the moves that make up the rhetorical structure of the proposal. It is a simple activity, for teenagers, but it fulfills the objective of raising awareness of the structure of the genre. Because it is a skills-integrated course, the writing activity is linked to the other activities in the lesson and springs from the topic of the reading, which is first worked on in its own right, with all the reading comprehension stages.

Below is a genre awareness activity at the advanced level[4]. The genre proposed in the writing prompt in the course book is a book review, but it does not provide a model and a genre analysis activity.

LEVEL: Advanced

Step 1: Setting the context: Students discuss how they choose books to read and whether or not they read book reviews, where they can find them, and how they are usually structured.

Step 2: Students read an authentic book review.

Step 3: Students answer the following questions about the book review.

1. Analyze the model. Look back at the model book review above and answer the following questions with your partner.
    a. What are some aspects of the text that make us identify it as a book review and not as an essay or an article?
    b. What exactly did the author write about?
    c. What questions does each paragraph answer?
       Introduction: _____
       Body: _____
       Conclusion: _____
    d. What words can you identify which represent the writer's opinion? How did he/she make the story sound appealing?
    e. Identify some vocabulary words related to books.
    f. What verb tense is mostly used? Why is it a preferred tense?

2. Focus on language: Go to your student's book page 18 and read the chart Linking Adjectives in Writing. Underline the adjective combinations the writer uses in the model review.

Now, with a partner, work on exercise B on page 18 of your student's book.

---

4. Created by Angela Minella, Casa Thomas Jefferson, Brasilia, Brazil.

The next stage in genre-based writing instruction is the joint construction stage, in which the teacher and the students construct a text together, using the knowledge gained from the awareness-raising activities. The teacher has the role of an interventionist, making sure the students understand and reproduce the typical rhetorical patterns of the genre. Nation (2009) calls these types of tasks shared tasks, and suggests that they can be done with the whole class, the teacher eliciting the sentences from the students and writing them on the board, or in groups. Hyland (2007) emphasizes the importance of collaboration and peer interaction in the joint construction stage, as well as the teacher's essential role of scaffolding the writing assignment in order to move students from their present level of knowledge to the intended level, thus creating what Vygostsky (1986) calls the *Zone of Proximal Development*.

In the writing lesson described above, after students have analyzed a proposal, the teacher leads them to construct a proposal together. They select a problem and the teacher elicits the sentences to construct the text from the students, focusing their attention on the different moves. This can be done on the board or with a word document projected on the board or a screen. If students have their own computers or smartphones with Internet connection, they can work together on a Google Doc.

The joint construction stage is a very important one in the scaffolding process. However, in a skills-integrated EFL classroom, time limitations may not allow teachers to engage students in the joint construction stage for all writing assignments. We must remember that we are not talking about a course dedicated exclusively to writing. If possible, then, the teacher should dedicate some time to joint construction in the first writing assignment, for example, but not necessarily all the others. Alternatively, the teacher can engage students in joint construction of a part of the text, such as the introduction, in one assignment, and then other parts of the text in other assignments. In the process-genre framework proposed here, the essential stage, one that should not be overlooked, is the genre awareness.

Here is a genre analysis activity[5] focused on a completely different genre, one that many teachers might not consider as a writing task because it is not "traditional" – a poster.

■ LEVEL: **Pre-intermediate**

Step 1: Students read three posters in the course book about different clubs that the students can join and answer comprehension questions.

Step 2: Students analyze the posters again and do the following task:

A good and effective poster needs to contain some basic elements. Answer the questions below with information from the posters in your book.

a. A poster should include a banner at the top with the title. What is the title of the first poster?
b. The purpose of the first poster is to advertise the Travel Club. What is the purpose of the second poster?
c. A good poster also has a sentence that introduces the topic. What is the introductory sentence in the third poster?
d. They also mention how they are going to guide the activities. For example, in the third poster, they are going to discuss how to plan a project and present it. How is the travel group going to work?

Step 3: Students talk about clubs and after-school activities at their school.

Step 4: Students are given a writing prompt: they are supposed to make a poster advertising a club offered at their school and are offered a framework for planning what to include in their poster.

Beyond analysis – explicit instruction

Though a very important stage of the writing process, leading students to notice genre features is not enough to help them acquire all the rhetorical tools they need to write effectively. They also need practice in using certain features, such as specific language structures, vocabulary, and cohesive devices. Thus, genre activities should also include practice, ranging from controlled to free. For

5. Created by Silvia Caldas, Casa Thomas Jefferson, Brasilia, Brazil.

example, after analyzing the types of cohesive devices used in a text, students can fill in the blanks of sentences with a set of connectors or practice using these connectors in sentences of their own. If the genre they analyzed favors passive voice constructions over active ones, students can practice changing sentences from active to passive voice. As it has been shown that academic texts are composed primarily of embedded noun phrases and prepositional phrases rather than clausal subordination (BIBER et al., 2011, p. 9), students can practice reducing restrictive relative clauses, as in the example below:

> The reaction to the question <u>that was posed</u> was very surprising.
> The reaction to the question <u>posed</u> was surprising.

Students should also receive explicit instruction related to how to vary sentence types in writing, how to make their sentences concise, and how to use more varied and low-frequency vocabulary in their texts. These activities should be linked to the genre analysis and spring from it.

The following stages of the genre teaching and learning cycle are students' redrafting and editing of their independent texts and receiving feedback. This is when students will produce their own texts, in the same genre as the one they analyzed, but on a different topic. Here is where a process-based approach, and its focus on the different stages of the writing process, can complement a genre-based approach. The genre analysis helps students identify the rhetorical structure of the genre they will need to produce. However, it does not necessarily help them with the content of their independent text. Thus, the pre-writing stage, in which students generate and organize ideas, is also an important stage in scaffolding students' writing, and it will be the focus of Chapter 4.

After your read

- Do the course books you use or are familiar with teach writing with a focus on genres the way it is presented in this chapter?
- Which of the guidelines proposed here would be easy to implement in your context and which ones would be difficult?

WRITING IS NOT ONLY A PERSONAL AND INDIVIDUAL ACTIVITY

Chapter 4
Generating ideas and planning

Before your read

- How do you usually generate ideas and plan for the writing you have to do in your daily life and professionally?
- Did you learn these techniques or do you follow them intuitively?
- Do you spend time in your class engaging students in activities for generating ideas and planning before you ask them to write?

After students have analyzed a model and developed genre awareness, they are given the task of producing their own text. Even though the model analysis and genre awareness activities helped them identify **how** to write their text, they need help in deciding **what** to write. Thus, it is very important to engage students in activities that will help them generate ideas and then plan how they will display these ideas in their writing. When teachers scaffold the writing task fully, helping students structure their texts in terms or language, organization, and content, students will be confident about their ability to perform the task. This also helps develop in students a more positive attitude towards writing than they usually have because it is more likely that they will be successful.

Ideally, generating ideas and planning should be carried out in the classroom, so that students can benefit from the collaborative construction of ideas with their peers and the teacher.

Generating ideas

The objective of idea-generation activities is to help students brainstorm what they can include in their writing, not necessarily how and in what order. There are many techniques for generating ideas and it is important for the teacher to explore a wide range of activities in their classes so that students have the chance to experiment with these different techniques and, eventually, become aware of which ones are more in keeping with their style. Different people prefer different methods, and in our goal of leading students to eventually become independent writers, we need to help students identify what works best for them.

Here we separate techniques for generating ideas from those for planning because it is important that, in the idea-generation stage, students not judge the ideas or worry about how they are going to sequence them in the text. The purpose is to come up with ideas that may or may not be used in the text itself. Planning comes later.

1 Brainstorming

The quintessential method for generating ideas is brainstorming. Students can be instructed to write down words or phrases that come to mind when they think about the topic proposed. For example, in Chapter 3, a genre awareness activity regarding a proposal for a charity request was presented. The proposal analyzed is a model and students are asked to write their own proposal. The next stage, then, before students begin to write, is to think about what to write. In the brainstorming stage, they can make a list of organizations that need help. They might start individually and then work in groups to share the lists they came up with. The teacher can also ask students to write the organizations on the board, so that students can broaden their perspective and perhaps write a proposal for an organization that they hadn't even thought of.

Brainstorming can be used not only to generate ideas, but also to generate key words that can be used in the task proposed. For example, students can analyze the model to identify the words that can be used in any text of the same genre and then they can come up with other words that they can use in their own text. Working collaboratively is very important because students are then not limited to their own ideas, but rather, to the ideas that have come up in class, in their collective construction.

2 Researching

For the same writing task proposed above – writing a proposal on how to help a charity – students need not limit themselves to the charities or organizations that they are already familiar with, but rather, they can research organizations around them. Nowadays, with the proliferation of smartphones and the greater availability of Internet access, it is easy to engage students in this research in class. The teacher can also use this opportunity to teach students how to do research on the Internet and judge the sources they come across.

3 Answering questions

Some types of writing activities, especially narratives, lend themselves better to the technique of providing students with questions whose answers will be

41

the content of the text. Suppose students are working on an accident report for an insurance company. After going through the genre analysis stage, they need to think about what accident to report. They can be given a set of questions to guide their thinking:

- Where were you?
- Who were you with?
- What happened?
- Whose fault was it?
- Was anyone injured?
- What was the damage to the vehicle?
- Did you collect the other driver's information?
- What did you do right after the accident?

If the narrative is on a more personal level, such as a scary, surprising, life-changing experience, the teacher can play soft music and ask students to close their eyes and remember the experience. The teacher slowly asks the questions and students think about them. When the music stops, students write everything they thought about on a piece of paper.

Another way of doing this is to have students themselves come up with the questions. This is suggested in Menasche (2013). Students write their topic sentences on a sheet of paper or index card. The teacher collects the cards or papers and redistributes them. Peers write questions related to the topic. This can be done in various rounds, so that each person interacts with three or four topics or even more, depending on the time available. Alternatively, the students can be asked to write only one question and pass the card or paper on to the next person, making the activity more dynamic.

4 Debating

This technique is very useful for writing tasks that require presenting both sides of an argument. Students can be presented with a statement and divide themselves between those who agree with the statement and those who disagree. Then they come up with arguments in favor of their point of view and write them down. After that, they engage in a debate, which can be done with the whole class or in pairs or groups. To help students develop the ability to think about a topic from a different perspective, they can be asked to defend a point of view that is opposite from theirs.

5   Talking about the topic

Sometimes the topic does not require looking at both sides of an issue, but rather, just thinking about what to write, such as in a narrative. Students can gain ideas by talking to each other freely about what they could write about and the details they could include. This can be done informally and without the need to fill out a form at first. Social interaction is a great way to organize thoughts and should be encouraged at all times in the classroom.

6   Free writing

Not all writers like to brainstorm ideas and write them down before they write. Some writers generate ideas as they write, so a very important technique for students to practice is free writing. In free writing, students are asked to write about their topic non-stop, for a certain number of minutes. They should be instructed not to take their pencils of pens off the sheet of paper and to write everything that comes to their mind on their topic. It is different from brainstorming because brainstorming produces a list, whereas free writing produces sentences that are somehow linked to one another.

After the free writing stage, students can work in pairs and take turns reading what they wrote to each other and asking questions that can further address the topic at hand. This way, students help one another come up with more ideas for their text.

Planning

After students have come up with ideas, they need to decide how they will organize them in their writing. There are some useful techniques for this and, again, students should be presented with a variety of techniques so they can experiment with them and decide which one works best for them.

1 Outlining

Perhaps the most traditional way of organizing ideas is by way of an outline. The outline is particularly useful for expository types of texts. The traditional outline for an argumentative or expository paragraph, for example, is shown in Figure 4.1.

1. Topic sentence
    a. Supporting sentence 1
        i. Detail 1a
        ii. Detail 1b
        iii. Detail 1c
    b. Supporting sentence 2
        i. Detail 2a
        ii. Detail 2b
        iii. Detail 2c
    c. Supporting sentence 3
        i. Detail 3a
        ii. Detail 3b
        iii. Detail 3c
2. Conclusion

Figure 4.1 – Outline structure

Students can write an outline of the model text analyzed and then write an outline for their own text. They can also give feedback on each other's outlines, with suggestions of what to add.

Not all genres are organized this way, though, so the structure of the outline can vary according to the genre. For example, in the genre analysis activity shown in Chapter 3, the students were asked to identify the different moves of the proposal:

» State the problem identified.
» Propose that the class/community help solve the problem.

» State how the class/community can help.
» Restate the problem and the outcome of the proposed action.

This structure that was used for genre analysis can also serve as the outline for students' writing.

Another way of doing something similar to an outline is completing a chart about what to include in the text. In Chapter 3, a genre analysis activity focused on posters was presented. Here is the chart that students filled out in order to plan their posters:

Poster title:	
Organization: clear purpose (introductory sentence)	
Method or procedures to guide the activities	
Place where meetings will take place	
Design and layout: colors	
Heading and fonts	
Images to be used	

Figure 4.2 – Chart to organize ideas for poster

2 Mind mapping

A mind map is a visual representation of hierarchical information. It's a more visual and succinct outline where the writer writes words or phrases rather than sentences. Mind mapping is a very popular technique and it is usually done by drawing a box or circle in the middle of a page with the main topic and then arrows leading to other boxes or circles – the branches - to provide subtopics related to the main idea. Then additional boxes or circles – the sub-branches - stem from the subtopics to provide more details/examples. This way, the thoughts are organized visually and related information is interconnected, as shown in Figure 4.3.

Mind-mapping can be used for both generating and organizing ideas at the same time, though it does force the writer not only to think about the ideas but also to establish relationships between them. Its advantage is that it saves time.

Graphic organizers are types of mind maps directed to a specific rhetorical structure, such as chains of events, looking at both sides of an issue, or describing a cycle, as shown in Figures 4.4 to 4.6 (WEST VIRGINIA DEPARTMENT OF EDUCATION). After the debate proposed above, for example, students can use the graphic organizer in Figure 5 to write down the ideas presented in the debate that they would like to use in their text.

These are only some examples of the many types of graphic organizers that can be used for writing. In fact, there are several websites and applications for mind maps and graphic organizers. A well-known, free, and easy to use iPad and web-based app is called Popplet (popplet.com) and it allows students to draw the boxes and arrows with their fingers and insert the words or phrases in them.

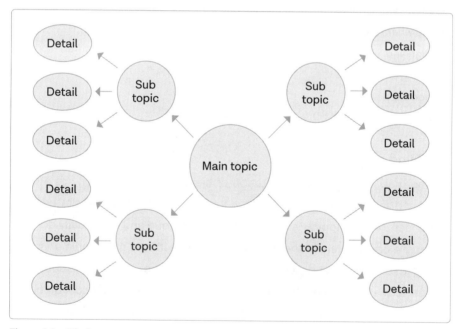

Figure 4.3 – Mind map

Generating ideas and planning

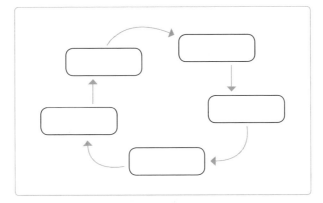

Figure 4.4 – Graphic organizer to demonstrate a cycle

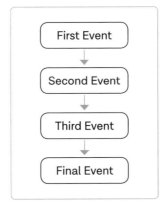

Figure 4.5 – Graphic organizer for chain of events

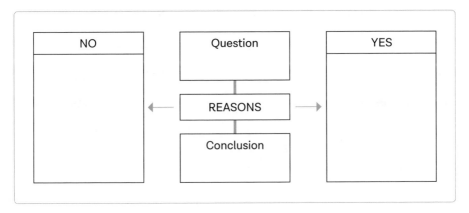

Figure 4.6 – Graphic organizer for looking at both sides of an issue

47

Teaching EFL writing – A practical approach for skills-integrated contexts

A. Christopher Columbus discovered America and became a fundamental man in history. Sometimes we know people who have done important things, too, but they don't become famous for that. Think about someone in your family or a friend's family who has done or achieved something you consider great or significant and write about it. Use the space below to brainstorm some ideas:

E.g. My grandmother got an award for Best Storyteller.
   My sister created a group that rescues stray cats and dogs in our neighborhood.
1. _____
2. _____
3. _____

B. Share your ideas with a partner.

C. At home, talk to your family and do some research. Use the cluster below to organize ideas before writing.

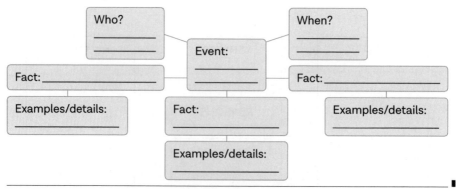

6. Created by Silvia Caldas, Casa Thomas Jefferson, Brasilia, Brazil.

Conclusion

Most of the time, the stage of the writing process most lacking in course book writing assignments is the generating ideas and planning one. We take for granted that just providing a model is sufficient orientation. However, the model only helps students identify the genre they will need to write in and how it is structured; it does not help students generate ideas for their own texts. If teachers follow the guidelines in this chapter, students will feel much more self-confident about their writing and will construct a better product.

So far, then, students have been provided with a context and purpose for writing, analyzed the genre they will have to write in, and engaged in activities to generate and plan ideas. Now students are ready to produce their first draft. The following chapter will talk about what is done after students have produced their first draft.

After your read

- Were you already familiar with all the techniques presented here? If so, how often do you use them in your own writing? If not, which ones would you like to start using?
- Which of these techniques do you think is more useful for your students?
- Do you agree that students should become familiarized with a wide range of techniques for generating ideas and planning? Justify your answer.
- Considering your teaching context, do you find it feasible to adopt and adapt some of the suggestions provided in this chapter?

Chapter 5

Peer feedback

Before your read

- When you have written something important, do you seek other people's help to revise it?
- Is it common in your context for teachers to have students give feedback on each other's writing? Why or why not? Have you ever had this experience as a student?
- Do you use peer feedback in your class? If so, does it work well? If not, would you be willing to try it? What would be some barriers you would face?

In a product approach to teaching writing, students write their texts, submit them to the teacher, and receive a grade. In this approach, the purpose of writing is not to develop writing skills, but rather, to verify whether students have acquired these skills. Conversely, in a process-based approach, the writing activity is regarded as a learning opportunity, a way of taking students from their current level of expertise to a higher level, with scaffolding and explicit intervention from the teacher. Writing is seen as a process with many stages that are not linear, but rather, recurrent.

One of these stages is drafting. In real life, when we need to write something upon which we will somehow be judged or that will lead to the attainment of a specific purpose, we make sure that the final product is as good as it can be. To this end, not only do we study similar types of writing – genres – and plan what we are going to write, but we also write a first draft and revise it based on our own self-assessment of the text and/or the assessment of others. If it is a high-stakes situation, we will most probably have another pair of eyes read our text and provide feedback. We and our reviser are also likely to focus on the content and organization of the writing the first time we read, make changes regarding these aspects, and then revise one more time to edit the text, that is, to tackle aspects related to language use and mechanics.

This real-life process of drafting and revising writing should be part of the EFL class. Ideally, especially from the intermediate level on, students should write two drafts before the final product – one in which only content and organization of ideas are addressed in the feedback, and another one for editing. A distinction is being made here between revising the piece of writing and editing it. Revision addresses the macro-level of the text and focuses on content, organization, and language use aspects that affect the comprehensibility of the text. Editing is more limited and is about re-reading the text to make sure it contains correct grammar, word choice, punctuation, and spelling. The argument in favor of focusing on the macro level first, rewriting the text, and then focusing on micro-elements, is that there is no use giving feedback on form on the first draft if students will have to change its content and organization anyway. It is indeed paradoxical to correct students' grammar, punctuation, and word choice in a paragraph and, at the same time, provide orientation on how to enrich the content of such paragraph, delete information that is not relevant, and/or reorganize it. In following the suggestions for improvement, students will certainly have to change the sentences and, thus, the corrections on form will be useless.

However, in a skills-integrated EFL context, writing is only one of the four skills focused on, besides the subskills of grammar and vocabulary, and students will probably have other assignments besides writing. Thus, the teacher and/or course developer will have to decide whether to engage students in a smaller number of writing assignments and have them write at least three versions of their text (two drafts plus the final piece), or include more writing assignments with two versions only (one draft and the final piece). The choice here is between depth and breadth. Working on fewer assignments more deeply will allow students to make more substantial improvements in their texts. Conversely, working a little more superficially on a larger number of assignments will allow students to experience producing texts in a wider variety of genres and experiment with a wider variety of writing techniques, rhetorical structures, and even language resources. This is really a choice the language program and the teachers need to make.

How to make peer feedback work

Regardless of whether students revise and edit their writing only once or if they do it twice, first focusing on content and organization and then focusing on form, another decision also has to be made: who will give feedback on students' drafts? Experienced writers are quite capable of revising and editing their own writing, even though most are eager to receive feedback from a peer. EFL students are not experienced writers in English and definitely need feedback. The most logical person to receive feedback from is the teacher. But should the teacher be the only source of feedback? The answer is no, for students can and should be encouraged to give feedback on each other's writing. Thus, both peer and teacher feedback should be built into the writing assignments.

Peer feedback, also called peer revision, is very common in writing classrooms in the United States, for example, but is rarely adopted in skills-integrated EFL classrooms, judging from the absence of this stage in the writing assignments presented in most course books. There are many reasons why EFL teachers may be resistant to peer revision in their skills-integrated classrooms:

» It is not a writing course, so we don't need to follow all the steps and procedures of a writing course.
» There is little time to work on writing in the skills-integrated classroom, let alone work with peer revision.
» Students don't like peer revision because they don't like to criticize their peer's work.
» Students are not capable of giving effective feedback to their peers.
» Students don't care about the feedback given by their peers.
» It is difficult to operationalize the activities when not all students bring their assignments to class on the due date.
» What students really want is feedback from the teacher.

On the other hand, there are also just as many very compelling reasons to adopt peer revision of writing even in the skills-integrated, EFL classroom, adapted from TSUI and NG (2000):

» It is in keeping with authentic social practices of writing, in which people spontaneously seek feedback from peers on their writing.
» It fosters a sense of audience, since students write not only for the teacher but also for the peers.
» It is one more opportunity for students to engage in genre awareness activities, this time analyzing a peer's text.
» It encourages collaborative learning and adds a social-interactive element to the writing assignment, reinforcing even further the integration of skills.
» It strengthens students' awareness of their strengths and weaknesses, as they compare their ability to tackle the writing assignment and their peers'.

- It strengthens students' ownership of texts.
- It takes away the focus from the teacher as the only source of knowledge in the classroom.

Nation (2009) adds that in the academic world, peer review is a relevant part of the publication process. The focus here is on peer revision, with primary attention given to content and organization, rather than on peer editing, in which the primary focus is on form. It is very limiting and misleading to ask students to read each other's pieces and focus primarily on language use. First, when we read a text for the first time, we focus our attention on what the writer has to say. Thus, this should be our first focus in peer revision. Second, the main objective of peer revision is to help writers improve their writing skills, not only their ability to use language correctly. Third, students are not always capable of identifying language errors in their peer's writing. Many times they correct what is right and overlook what is wrong. There can be an editing element in the peer review activity, but it shouldn't be limited to a mere editing activity.

For peer revision to work effectively, the teacher needs to follow some important, practical tips:

1 Begin small

One of the biggest mistakes teachers can make is to be too ambitious and want to have students revise their peers' writing like pros. We have to understand that it is hard even for teachers to decide what to focus on and to provide effective feedback to students. The suggestion is to choose a few points to focus on and to prioritize macro elements of writing, rather than small details. For example, students can be asked to verify if the paragraph has a topic sentence, at least three different arguments to support it, and a conclusion that restates the thesis. This can be done with a short checklist. Nation (2009) corroborates this suggestion by recommending that the reviewer focus on one or two aspects of the piece of writing.

2   Start with written feedback

In cultures in which students are not used to providing feedback to each other, having students sit face to face and talk about one another's writing can be daunting. The natural tendency to save face will prevail and the feedback will not be productive. According to Nation (2009), the quality of peer feedback is enhanced when students are provided with written guidelines to use during the evaluation. It doesn't mean that face-to-face feedback should be avoided. Quite the contrary: it should be our ultimate goal, but we have to train students to reach this stage.

3   Use a peer review sheet

In many cultures, students don't like it when their peers write comments on their paper or make corrections. Likewise, peer reviewers are reluctant to write on their peers' sheets. It is thus recommendable to always use a separate peer review sheet with questions addressing what you want to focus on, such as a checklist.

4   Customize your peer review sheet for the writing task at hand and the age of the learners

Don't use a general form for every piece of writing. The peer revision focus will also vary according to the genre and the specific writing subskill you are focusing on. For example, if it's a descriptive piece, you will necessarily want to address whether the writer has used a variety of adjectives to portray vividly whatever it is they are describing. For younger learners, you can use smiling faces or sad faces and include very simple elements such as whether the first paragraph is indented, if there are periods at the end of each sentence, or if the writer addressed all the questions in the pre-writing task, for example.

5   Make sure you include feedback on the ideas, not just the writing

The ultimate reason why we read what other people write is not to give feedback on the quality of the writing per se, but rather, because we are interested in what the writer has to say. Though the purpose of the peer revision activity is to provide feedback on the writing, make sure you add an item or two about what the writer has to say. Questions such as "Do you agree with the writer's point of view?" or "Does the writing make you want to visit the place being described?" should also be part of the peer review sheet.

6   Model the activity with the whole class

The ability to provide effective feedback on writing is not innate and it is likely that students will not have experienced this pedagogical practice in their regular schooling. Hence, we have to teach this to our students. The best way to do it is to model the peer review task with the whole class. You can ask a fellow teacher for an anonymous piece of writing on the same topic, but by a student from another class, and project the writing for everyone to see. Hand out the peer review form and elicit responses from students as you fill out a collective form. Alternatively, students can work in pairs or groups to fill out the peer review sheet and then whole-class debriefing can ensue. Students need this type of scaffolding. Min (2006 as cited in Nation, 2009) demonstrates that training learners in doing peer revision leads to better revisions.

7   Start with anonymous feedback

This may be arguable, but students feel less intimidated when they provide anonymous feedback to an anonymous writer. Later on, when students gain more confidence, they can start by exchanging papers with someone they feel comfortable with. At a third stage, when this type of activity has become a more natural step in the class, they accept exchanging papers with less familiar classmates. Having students from different groups of the same level revise each other's writing works well, too.

8   Vary your peer revision activities

It is advisable to start with a checklist, a simple, straightforward way to verify if the writing fulfills the basic requirements. Then you can move on to a mixed form, with a checklist and one or two open-ended questions. After that, you can add more and more open-ended questions until students are ready to even suggest what they should look for in the writing. We can really be sure that students have become competent peer reviewers when they can just read each other's writing, look each other in the eyes, and provide honest, constructive, non-judgmental feedback in a symmetrical conversation. It takes time, effort, and a lot of modeling to reach this stage, but it is possible. Also, make sure you focus on different aspects of writing, such as organization of ideas, how ideas are linked between sentences and between paragraphs, the use of low-frequency words, etc. The genre will also naturally dictate what to focus on in the peer revision.

9 Validate the peers' comments in your own comments

Peer feedback does not substitute teacher feedback. Of course, when students are seasoned peer reviewers, you can provide your feedback at a later stage of the process. Until then, collect the pieces of writing with the corresponding peer review sheet and add your comments to the peer's comments. When you agree with the peer reviewer, make sure you mention that. This validates the peer's feedback and makes the writer more confident to follow the suggestion.

10 Be consistent and persistent

If you decide that peer revision of writing is a stage of the writing process that you value and want to include in your lesson plan, make sure you do it in all your writing activities. Be aware that it might not work well the first time and that students will probably complain the first few times you do it, but it will slowly become a natural, transparent phase in your procedures if you are persistent enough. Don't give students mixed messages by doing peer revision with some writing tasks but not with others.

As Liu and Hansen (2002, p. 27) conclude their chapter addressing what research has shown about the effects of peer response,

> [...] peer response can be effective in helping learners develop their writing skills through interacting with other readers/writers, reading others' work, getting others' perspectives on their own work, and negotiating about

content and rhetorical and grammatical issues. Students are able to give specific feedback regarding content and rhetorical and grammatical issues, which is valued and employed successfully in revision, especially if students have undergone instruction in how to respond to their peer's papers.

Examples of peer feedback activities

Peer feedback activities can range from very simple ones, such as reading a peer's paper and reacting to its content by answering a question or completing a sentence, to more complex and multi-layered ones in which the reviser focuses on content, rhetoric, and language use. Below are three general types of tools that can be used in peer revision activities, progressing from controlled to free, open-ended ones.

1   Checklists

As suggested above, checklists are perhaps the first tool to use when students are not familiar with peer feedback. The checklist clearly directs the reviewer's attention to the relevant features in the text. It also eliminates any subjective judgment that may frighten novice peer reviewers.

The most traditional type of checklist enumerates the well-known elements of an essay and can be used to assess any text of this genre. The most effective checklists, though, are those that are customized for the writing task at hand, considering its objectives and guidelines.

Since students should write different genres, the checklist can also be directly linked to the genre awareness activity carried out in the beginning of the writing process. For example, in the activity presented in Chapter 3, students had to analyze the moves in the proposal. These same moves can be analyzed by the students in their peer's texts:

Which of the steps below can you identify in your peer's text?
a. ____ The writer explains what the problem is.
b. ____ The writer proposes a solution to the problem.
c. ____ The writer concludes by restating the problem and the outcome of the proposed action.

The peer review activity can be as simple as the checklist above, or it can include other elements, focusing on other writing subskills:

Check which of these requirements you think your peer fulfilled in the text:
_____ Use of descriptive vocabulary related to the topic and learned in the lesson.
_____ Use of connectors to link ideas.
_____ Use of correct grammar and punctuation.

It can also include a qualitative comment about the text:

Is it an effective proposal, that is, does it make you as a reader want to contribute to the organization proposed by the writer? Justify your answer.

Here is an example of a peer review sheet designed to be used with students who had never conducted this type of activity. First, the teacher projected a student sample on the board and went over each item on the checklist, eliciting from students whether the sample writing fulfilled each of the objectives stated on the checklist. After this modeling, each student was given a text written by a peer and asked to fill out the form.

You are going to be the reviewer of your friend's composition. Your job is to help your friend see what he/she has done well and how he/she do an even better job. Read your friend's composition carefully and check (✓) the points that you can identify in it.

Content and Organization:
( ) The composition has three paragraphs.

( ) The first paragraph explains who the person is and why he/she is stressed.
( ) In the first paragraph, there are a lot of examples of behaviors that show how stressed the person is.
( ) The second paragraph gives suggestions of what the person should do to become more relaxed.
( ) In the second paragraph, there are many ideas of how the person should relax, followed by details and examples.
( ) The third paragraph talks about how stressed or relaxed the writer is and how he/she can help his/her friend / relative / boss / etc.
( ) In the third paragraph, there are a lot of examples of why the writer is stressed or relaxed.
( ) The ideas in the composition are linked effectively with words like **and**, **but**, **because, to start with, in my opinion, for example, also**, etc.

Vocabulary
( ) The writer used some of the words learned in Unit 2.

Grammar
( ) The writer used adverbs of frequency.
( ) The writer used adverbs of frequency correctly.
( ) The writer used verb tenses correctly.
( ) The writer used the "s" in verbs in the simple present after he/she.

Make a compliment to your friend about his/her composition. In other words, what did your friend do particularly well in his composition?

_____
_____
_____
_____

Depending on how much time the teacher has for the peer review activity, how ready the teacher thinks students are for the task, and the intended focus, the peer review sheet can contain some or all the stages exemplified above.

Teaching EFL writing – A practical approach for skills-integrated contexts

2   Questionnaires

Once students are a bit more familiarized with the task of revising their peers' writing, the peer review activity can slowly become less and less controlled, with both a checklist and open-ended questions, as shown in the example below, a peer review sheet about a narrative text.

I. Read your friend's story and write a general comment about it, the way an interested reader does. Don't just say, "I like your story." React to it!

II. Now check if the narrative has all the elements below:
( ) It has at least three paragraphs.
( ) The first paragraph gives background information about the story, that is, where the narrator was and what he/she was doing.
( ) The second paragraph describes the experience.
( ) The third paragraph wraps up the story, that is, it makes a general comment about the experience.
( ) There are at least five connectors.
( ) The story is told in the past, with verbs in the past.
( ) The writer used at least some more expressive – versus common – words (e.g. "amazing" instead of "good")

III. Every story can be told in a richer way if the narrator adds details to make it more interesting and involving. Write three questions that you think your friend could answer to make the narrative richer in details.

In this peer review activity, students are asked to react to the content of the narrative, decide if it contains all the elements required in the assignment, and ask questions to help the writer enrich the text. The types of items on the peer review sheet can vary depending on the teacher's goal and the time available. The peer review sheet can contain many tasks, only a few, or even just one, depending on the context.

Here is another example of a more open-ended peer review activity, based on a piece intermediate-level teenagers wrote for the school blog about their favorite children's book.

Peer feedback

Read your classmate's book review and answer the questions below:

1. What do you think of the writer and book/comic book/ story your classmate wrote about? Have you heard of him/her? Have you read the book/ comic book/ story?

2. Does your classmate's text make you interested in and curious about reading the book? Why/Why not?

3. Did your classmate follow the outline suggested (see the outline below)?

a. Paragraph 1
- Are there many writers of children's books in Brazil?
- Who are they?
- Who are the most famous ones?
- Which one is your favorite? Why?
- Which is your all-time favorite book?

b. Paragraph 2
- Who are the main characters in your all-time favorite?
- What is the story about?
- What's the best part?
- What's its saddest part?

c. Paragraph 3
- What was the moral of the story?
- Do you agree with it? Why?

4. If not, which of the part(s) above was/were not included? Even so, is the writing effective, that is, did the writer follow another outline that was effective?

5. Write here all the linking words that your classmate used. Were they enough within the framework of the context as a whole, or do you think he/she should add more linking words?

6. Did your classmate use effective and varied vocabulary, only simplistic vocabulary (only basic-level words) or generally effective vocabulary?

7. What did you learn from reading your classmate's composition that you can apply to your own composition?

63

This peer review activity requires more critical thinking and experience with peer revision. It also goes one step further in that it asks students to reflect upon how they could improve their own writing based on reading how a peer addressed the same task.

3 Structured conversations

Once students have gained practice in giving feedback to peers based on a checklist and then on a more open-ended questionnaire, they are ready to engage in a structured conversation with their peers regarding the piece of writing at hand. A simple and effective way to structure this conversation is to have students give concrete examples regarding the strengths and weaknesses of the text. As they have practiced giving feedback using more guided activities, they will have developed an awareness of what to focus on and what language to use in this feedback. If time allows, the teacher can scaffold the task by eliciting from students what they think is important to pay attention to when giving feedback on a peer's writing and write what students say on the board. This can serve as a student-generated guide for the peer feedback.

After listening to their peer's feedback, students can then complete a simple chart with the comments made, to make sure they have understood all the comments, and also to have them available when rewriting the text.

Positive points	Points that need improvement

The type of language used in the peer review activities will also depend on students' age and proficiency level. Liu and Hansen (2002, p. 51) present examples of guiding questions for peer response with school-age writers (Table 5.1).

Table 5.1 – Guiding questions for peer response with younger learners

	PRIMARY LEVEL	MIDDLE SCHOOL LEVEL	SECONDARY LEVEL
Content	What part of the story did you like the best? Why? What part of the story didn't you understand?	What interested you most in the story? What part of the story did you want the writer to add more details to?	What part of the story was the most vivid to you? Why? What part of the story needed more details and/or action?
Rhetoric	Did the story have an ending?	What is the climax of the story? Does the action lead up to the climax? How?	Who was the narrator of the story? Did you get a clear idea of how the narrator felt about the events in the story?
Grammar/ style	Are all the words spelled correctly? Are the first words in every sentence capitalized?	Are there any spelling errors in the paper? Any grammar errors? Please circle any misspelled words and underline any grammatical errors.	Are there any spelling errors in the paper? Any grammar errors? Please circle any misspelled words and underline any grammatical errors.

Source: LIU and HANSEN, 2002, p. 50.

Peer feedback in earlier stages of the writing process

The section above focused on ways to engage students in the revision of their peers' first drafts. However, peer revision can also occur in earlier stages of the writing process. For example, when students are planning what to write and how to organize it, they may write an outline or complete a mind map. Students can be asked to exchange papers and give feedback on their peer's plan, based on guidelines provided by the teacher.

For an essay outline, for example, the peer can be asked to check if the thesis statement has a controlling idea and if all the topic sentences are directly linked to the thesis. They can also check if the writer listed enough details and examples to support each of the topic sentences. Giving feedback at this stage also allows students to suggest how their peers can address the topic more effectively.

In a free writing task, as already suggested in Chapter 4, students can exchange papers and suggest how they could enrich the text. This can be done by way of questions. The activity benefits both the writer and the peer reviewer, as reading how a peer plans to address a topic can help the reviewer gain insights for their own writing.

This chapter has focused on strategies for peer revision, based on the premise that students can perform at their best when they work collaboratively. Also, by giving feedback on their peer's writing, students also learn to become better reviewers of their own writing. The following chapter focuses on how the teacher can effectively complement the peer's feedback, also exploring different paths that can be followed depending on the context.

After your read

- Which of the activities suggested here would be easy for you to implement?
- Which one(s) would be challenging? Why?
- Do you now feel compelled to implement or to continue using peer feedback in your class?

WRITING IS SEEN AS A PROCESS WITH MANY STAGES THAT ARE NOT LINEAR

Chapter 6

Teacher feedback

Before your read

- In your experiences writing for school, how have teachers typically given feedback on your writing?
- In which ways was this feedback effective and in which ways was it ineffective?
- What is the greatest challenge you face as a teacher when you have to give feedback on your students' writing?

There is some controversy regarding whether students should receive feedback from a peer and from the teacher on the same draft, as students might tend to focus on the teacher's feedback and ignore the peer's (LIU and HANSEN, 2002). Ideally, then, peer feedback and teacher feedback should be given on different drafts, with peer feedback on the first draft and teacher feedback on the second. However, in a skills-integrated EFL context, this may not always be possible. In this case, the teacher can mitigate this problem by providing feedback that complements the peer's and avoid overlaps. For example, if the peer has already pointed out a weakness in organization, the teacher does not need to point the same thing out again. In fact, the teacher can corroborate the peer's feedback, writing "I agree" next to the peer's comment, for example. The teacher's role, then, is to revise the peer's feedback and point out what the peer has overlooked.

Another controversy regards whether students should receive simultaneous feedback on both content and form. According to some composition theorists, premature feedback on form can "short-circuit students' ability to think, compose and revise their content" (FERRIS, 2002, p. 49). Also, if students receive feedback on form in an earlier stage of the composing process, in which they are still deciding what to say, they will shift their attention from content to form and their writing tasks become a proofreading exercise, rather than a composing one (SOMMERS, 1982; ZAMEL, 1982, as cited in FERRIS, 2002). However, Ferris mentions studies that have indicated that students benefit from simultaneous feedback on content and form and argues that not providing any feedback on form on the first draft misses the opportunity to provide feedback at a teachable moment. It seems to be a disservice to students to have them repeat the same mistake in multiple drafts before finally addressing this mistake. Ferris suggests providing general feedback about form on preliminary drafts, together with comments on content and organization.

However, Ferris' (2002) focus is on specific writing courses. In a skills-integrated program in which students have other tasks to perform besides writing, it may not be possible to engage students in writing multiple drafts.

In this case, teachers have no choice, but to provide simultaneous feedback on content, organization, and form.

Practical guidelines for effective teacher feedback

Teachers' natural tendency when they are faced with the task of "correcting" a student's piece of writing is to grab a pen, start reading, and immediately correct students' errors. The problem with this habit is that teachers end up focusing primarily on form and run the risk of making corrections that are not appropriate because they did not read the whole text.

Here are the recommended steps for tackling the challenging task of giving feedback on students' writing.

1. Read the whole text, with pen or pencil down – or the mouse, if you are using a computer. You need to focus on what the student had to say and not on how they said it. It is difficult at first, especially if the writing is filled with errors.
2. Write an end comment reacting to what the student had to say, that is, the communicative purpose of the text. This establishes a personal and emotional connection with the writer.
3. Read the text again, now focusing on specific content and organization. If a peer revision activity was conducted and there is an accompanying peer review sheet, go through the peer reviewer's analysis. Do you agree? If so, make a note of it. If there were aspects in content and organization that the peer reviewer overlooked, comment on them.
4. Write comments regarding content and organization on the margins. Make sure your comments are text-specific. If the content is not rich enough, ask questions that will prompt students to enrich the text. Do not write general comments such as "you need to provide more information" or "not clear". Be specific about what information the student needs to provide and about what exactly is not clear in the sentence or groups of sentences. Nowadays, with the use of technology, students can write their texts electronically

and the teacher can give feedback on the word or the Google document. Alternatively, you can record your comments. If you are using Google Classroom, for example, you can use a recording plug-in to provide oral feedback on your students' writing. If the writing is done by hand, make sure your comments on the margins are clear and well organized. If there are too many comments for the margins, you can number the comments on the margins and write them at the end, after the general comment on content.

5   There are two ways to approach the next stage, depending on whether the teaching context allows for the writing of two or more drafts and the final product or of only one draft and then the final product.

- a   If the student will have the chance to write more than one draft and this is the first one, write general feedback on form. For example, if the text is a narrative and the student kept shifting from present to past tense, you can write "decide if you want to narrate your story in the present or in the past and stick to it". If the text contains many fragments, you can write "please revise your text for fragments". You might also need to explain what a fragment is and give an example. This will allow the student to write the second draft with these general guidelines in mind. For this second draft, use the guidelines below.
- b   If you don't have time to work on multiple drafts and this is the only draft the student will write before the final one, then you need to provide specific feedback on form. In this case, students will receive both feedback on content and organization and feedback on form in the same draft. Just make sure you do not give feedback on form in parts that you suggest that the student change completely or delete. Also, it is useful to write a general comment about error patterns that you identified throughout the text, such as: "You will see that I pointed out many mistakes in word forms. Analyze your sentences more carefully to decide if the word you want to use should be a noun, an adjective, an adverb or a verb."

6   If you followed the guidelines in 5.a. above, for the second draft, you will follow the steps in 5.b. In other words, the first draft will contain only

comments about content and organization and a general comment about form, while the second draft will contain specific feedback on form.
7   Make sure you balance positive and negative problems.

There are two types of feedback on form: direct and indirect. The direct feedback is the one in which the teacher underlines the mistake and already provides the correction. The indirect type of feedback is the one in which the teacher underlines the mistake for the student to correct or underlines the mistake and writes a code or a comment regarding what type of mistake it is. The advantage of indirect correction is that it places responsibility on the learner to find out what the correct form is, based on the teacher's guidelines, which may lead to more long-term retention. However, as Ferris (2002) points out, there are errors that students are not able to correct by themselves and that should, thus, be corrected directly by the teacher. These are usually errors of word choice and word form, as well as awkward or unidiomatic sentence structure. It might be more helpful for the teacher to suggest a different word than to underline the word and write "ww" (wrong word). While too much direct correction can lead to the teacher's appropriation of the student text and to the student's passive rewriting of the correct version, too much indirect correction can be overwhelming for students. It is best, then, to use both types of correction.

Below is a flow chart to help teachers decide what type of feedback to provide and how.

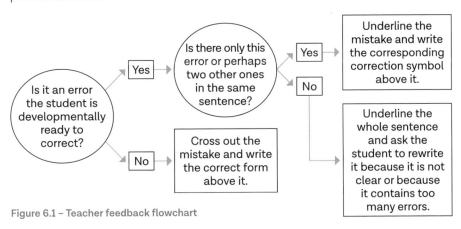

Figure 6.1 – Teacher feedback flowchart

The variety of correction symbols used will depend on the level. Table 6.1 presents a list of proofreading symbols that can be used at the intermediate and advanced levels, with examples. This list should be made available to students, and the teacher should go over the symbols with the students to make sure they understand each one, especially when it comes to discriminating between an error in verb tense (vt) or verb form (vf) or between a wrong word (ww) or a wrong word form (wf). While some may argue that this distinction may be confusing to students, who may not know the difference between a verb tense and a verb form, for example, it can actually prevent students from changing the wrong thing. For example, if a student writes - "I was walk to school when the accident happened" - and the teacher just underlines "was walk" and says it is a verb error, the student might feel compelled to change the tense altogether. However, if the teacher underlines only "walk" and writes "vf" above it, the student will clearly know that the tense – past continuous – is correct, and it is just the form – walk – that needs to be corrected. However, for this system to be effective, the teacher should have gone over the difference between the two with the whole class. Also, every time a draft with correction symbols is returned to students, it is advisable that students have some time to go over the corrections and comments in class and clarify any doubts they may have. This is also one more opportunity to engage students in peer revision. Students can consult with each other about how to correct the mistakes that have been pointed out.

* * *

Teacher feedback

Table 6.1 – Correction symbols

SYMBOLS	ERRORS	EXAMPLE MISTAKES	CORRECTION (DONE BY STUDENTS)
¶	Paragraph		
no ¶	No paragraph		
∧	Insert here	I'm tired ∧ going to the club.	I'm tired **of** going to the club.
a	Delete	He needs **a** money.	He needs **Ø** money.
(∧)	Transpose	I love ∧ cream **(ice)**.	I love **ice** cream.
sales()man	Connect	He's a **sales()man**.	He's a **salesman**.
a /lot	Separate	I work **a/lot**.	I work **a lot**.
—	Capital letter / Lowercase	He never works on **saturday**. He's from the **Capital** of Brazil.	He never works on **Saturday**. He's from the **capital** of Brazil.
rec**ie**ved sp	Spelling	He rec**ie**ved a check. sp	He **received** a check.
○ p	Missing punctuation	I love going out○I also like to stay at home.	I love going out**.** I also like to stay at home.
⊙ p	Wrong punctuation	John isn't feeling well**,** he's sick. p	John isn't feeling well**.** He's sick.
⊗ p	No punctuation	I study English**,** p because I like it.	I study English **Ø** because I like it.
vf	Wrong verb form	Mary (have) to travel vf today. He enjoys (to play) videogame. vf	Mary **has** to travel today. He enjoys **playing** videogame.
vt	Wrong verb tense	Mary (has) to travel *last* vt week.	Mary **had** to travel *last* week.
frag	Incomplete sentence; fragment	**Although I'm sick**. frag	**Although I'm sick, I can go to school.**

75

How ww	Wrong word	**How** you know, ww I'm from Brazil.	**As** you know, I'm from Brazil.
exciting wf	Word form	I am **exciting** about wf traveling. wf I have a lot of **friend**.	I am **excited** about traveling. I have a lot of **friends**.
of prep	Wrong preposition	It depends **of** her decision. **prep**	It depends **on** her decision.
id	Idiom (not expressed this way in English)	They **didn't have conditions** to go there. id	They **were not able** to go there.
poss	Use of possessive and apostrophe	My **friend** name is Mary. poss **He** name is John. poss	My **friend's** name is Mary. **His** name is John.
mod	Incorrect use or formation of a modal	You **mustn't** study so mod hard to get a…	You **don't have to** study so hard to get a good grade in the test.

Conferencing

Perhaps the most effective way to give feedback to a student on their writing is having a one-to-one conversation. This allows the teacher to explain the comments and corrections clearly, and the student can ask questions and seek help. Whether or not the teacher will be able to adopt conferencing for feedback depends on a number of factors, including size of the group, course schedule, role of writing in the course, students' age and, thus, disposition to work more independently while the conferences are taking place.

If the teacher is creative, though, students can be assigned a project or a collaborative activity in well-designed and motivating stages that will keep the students busy so that the teacher can be free to engage in private conversations with one student at a time. This might not be possible to do with every writing assignment, but it will be beneficial even if it is done only once per semester or term, preferably with the first writing assignment.

Using technology for feedback

Nowadays there is a vast variety of technology tools that can be used to facilitate and enhance the writing process. As mentioned earlier, students can write their texts using Microsoft Word or Google Docs, and the teacher can provide feedback on these documents rather than on a print version. For peer revision, the forms can be filled out online too, if there are resources for this. Especially with teens and young adults, it is advisable to do the peer revision in class, for students may not complete the task in a timely manner if it is assigned for home work, and this can jeopardize the flow of the whole writing cycle. However, each teacher must decide what fits their context and their students' profile better.

Teachers can go beyond using word processing documents and use other resources to enhance the teaching of all skills in general and writing in particular. Here are some examples, among many others that are available:

1. Google Classroom: Google Classroom is part of the Google Suite for Education and it is available free of charge, as long is your school is registered to use it. With Google Classroom, teachers can post assignments for students, keep track of their progress, and give feedback. All types of worksheets can be stored there for students' easy access, such as the writing assignments, peer review sheets, correction and proofreading symbols, etc. Students can contact the teacher via Google Classroom as well. There are a variety of apps that can be integrated into Google Classroom, including Kaisena (https://kaizena.com/), an app that allows the teacher to highlight parts of the student's text and record comments.
2. Microsoft Classroom: Microsoft also has its own version of a digital classroom, part of their Office 365 Education suite. Just like in Google Classroom, the teacher can manage the class, create, share and mark assignments, and use a variety of Office 365 tools to enhance learning. Kaisena also works with Office 365. Word's "track changes" and "compare

documents" features can be customized to aid in the feedback-giving process, too (NEGHAVATI, 2016).

3. Moodle: It is a free, open-access learning management system that can be used for online and blended courses. Managing the writing component on Moodle is also very convenient, and it has an activity called "Workshop" that works very well for peer revision, for the system itself will assign texts for peers to review, either according to the instructor's preference or randomly. It also has a built-in camera and microphone feature that teachers and students can use for oral feedback. Teachers can also use other Learning Management Systems to achieve the same goal.

4. Wikis: A wiki is a kind of website that allows for collaborative editing. It enables teachers and students to create content online using tools that are easy to understand. There is no need to know coding or understand the more technical aspects of websites to use wiki. Two well-known educational wiki sites are pbworks (http://www.pbworks.com/) and wikispaces (www.wikispaces.com). Both have specific solutions for teachers and schools and free packages. Each student can have a different page in the wiki and post all their drafts there. Peers can also give feedback easily. The teacher can have a page with the worksheets and proofreading symbols.

5. Video feedback platforms: There are a host of video recording platforms that can be used for teacher feedback. One of them is Jing (https://www.techsmith.com/jing.html), which allows you to screencast your feedback-giving process and then share this screencast with students.

6. Skype: Skype is a video-conferencing tool that can be used for the one-to-one conferences about writing. Skype allows the user to upload a file and share the screen, so the teacher can go over the writing with the student. There are other videoconferencing tools that can be used for the same purpose.

Teaching students to become independent editors

A common complaint among teachers is that they provide the same feedback over and over again and students keep making the same mistakes. Sometimes they feel that the students' learning process starts all over again each time they have a new assignment, and that learners do not transfer what they learned from earlier assignments to new ones. In order to guarantee longer-term retention and to teach students to self-edit, it is important for teachers to go beyond the feedback they give on individual assignments. Here are some ways in which they can do this.

1   Whole-class editing activity

After each writing assignment, collect the most common mistakes made and develop a worksheet with these errors. Have students work in pairs or groups to try to find out what the mistakes are and correct them. This can be made into a game, such as tic-tac-toe or Auction. This helps increase learners' awareness of errors and of the fact that their colleagues make the same mistakes they do, lowering their anxiety.

2   Guided self-editing

Based on the mistakes made by the students on previous assignments, the teacher can guide students through the self-editing process. The day they bring their first drafts to class, either on paper or electronically, students are asked to go over the assignment one more time, revising it for specific aspects listed by the teacher, such as "Read your text again and check if all the sentences contain a subject and a verb and express a complete idea", or "Read your text again and check that you did not connect two independent ideas, or clauses, with just a comma." Students can also receive an editing checklist and go over their writing to make sure all the items on the checklist were taken care of in the writing.

3 Error-tracking chart

The teacher can provide students with a chart that contains the different types of errors. The categories can be the same as the ones used in the correction symbols. The chart contains a column for each writing assignment. Students record how many mistakes they made in each category. This will help raise their awareness of their most common types of errors and track whether they are making progress. The chart can also address problems related to content and organization.

Giving feedback on students' writing is a painstaking task, and the teacher should use the resources available, including peers, to facilitate the process. Writing should not be regarded as a testing activity, but rather, as a learning one. Thus, it is important that students are given the opportunity to revise their texts to improve and, ultimately, become proficient and independent writers.

Now that we have gone over all the stages of the writing process and students have written multiple drafts and received feedback on them from both peers and the teacher, it is time to assess the writing, the topic of Chapter 7.

Table 6.2 – Error tracking chart

HOW MANY MISTAKES I MADE RELATED TO:	WRITING 1	WRITING 2	WRITING 3
Content			
Organization of ideas			
Use of discourse markers			
Fragments			
Run-ons			

Teacher feedback

Verb Tenses			
Verb forms			
Wrong word			
Word form			
Possessives			
Prepositions			
Idiomatic expressions			

After your read

- Which ideas in this chapter reflect what you already did when giving feedback to your students?
- Which ideas were new?
- Which if these ideas would you find easiest and most difficult to implement and why?

Chapter 7

Assessing student writing

Before your read

- In your experiences writing for school, how were your compositions assessed in most cases? Did the teacher simply give you a grade? If so, how did you interpret that grade? Were there other ways the teachers assessed you beyond giving a grade?
- If there is a writing component in the courses you teach, how do you assess your students' writing?
- Do you know what a rubric or rating scale is? Can you name the three general types?

In a process-genre approach, after peers and the teacher have given feedback on drafts, students produce what is called the final product and probably also expect feedback on it. However, since students will not have the chance to revise anymore, the feedback on the final product needs to have a different focus. Even if the writing assignment does not need to be formally graded, it does need to be assessed, for students need to know if they have met the criteria for the task. Assessment should not be confused with grading; you can assess without necessarily assigning a numerical figure to your assessment.

The feedback on the drafts has a more formative nature, providing assessment for learning. Conversely, the feedback, or assessment, of the final product takes a summative stance, that is, it is assessment of learning. It will sum up what students achieved at the end of the learning process, after the formative stage has been concluded. Working on writing by way of the process approach, giving feedback along the way, is a formative type of assessment because the students have the chance to learn from their mistakes and repeat the task, ideally until they achieve at least satisfactory results. The assessment done at the end of the process can be considered summative because it is carried out after the learning has taken place, but it can have a formative element if it also considers the progress students have made along the way. Besides, it has a highly formative element if it provides useful information about what the student has done well or not that can help with future writing assignments. In other words, the assessment at the end of the process can have a "feed-forward" nature if it is done effectively. Thus, the difference between formative and summative assessment does not lie on the assessment tools used, but rather, on how they are used. Summative and formative assessment should thus be seen as a continuum, rather than a binary distinction.

One way to assess the final product is to simply write comments about the criteria that have been achieved and the ones that haven't, if any. The focus should be on whether the writing meets the communicative purpose of its genre and the language use is appropriate for the student's proficiency level. This is a descriptive type of assessment and it is more informal in the sense that it does not use a formal instrument as a reference. However, it can be painstaking for the teacher to write comprehensive, individualized comments on each student paper, especially when many of the comments will be the same. Of course, individualization should be any teacher's priority, but for practical purposes, the teacher can use a general assessment instrument for the comments that will be the same and just add the individual comments.

What teachers should not do, though, is to simply provide a numerical grade on the assignment, without any type of explanation of how this grade was arrived at. It is also not advisable to divide the grade into categories, assign points to them, and simply specify how many points students received for each aspect, without further explanations, such as: Content, 8/10; Organization, 7/10; Language Use, 5/10; Vocabulary, 4/5; Mechanics, 4/5; Total, 33/40. This numerical feedback does not inform the student of what criteria were used to determine each of the points. What differentiates an 8 in content from a 10? What would a 10 look like? And an 8? These are old-fashioned practices in writing assessment that are not pertinent in contemporary second language writing instruction.

Scoring rubrics

The assessment instrument that provides criteria for writing and the degrees in which these criteria have been met is called a rubric. When numbers are assigned to the levels of achievement, to produce a final grade, it becomes a scoring rubric or a rating scale. These two terms are mostly used interchangeably, but Plakans and Gebril (2015) point out that a rating scale has the main purpose of determining a score and, thus, may provide less detail in criteria. A rubric is used for educational purposes and so the criteria and descriptors should be more transparent and concrete in order to fulfill the purpose of providing feedback to students.

A rubric does not necessarily have to produce a score, though. It can be only descriptive. This will depend on the course's assessment system and whether it contains a writing component or not. Ideally, assessment systems should encompass diverse types of assessment, and not only tests, which are considered a traditional type of assessment. Conversely, a writing task is a performance type of assessment. Thus, if students have to produce pieces of writing, and especially if they do so by way of a formative process, why not include these in the assessment system, rather than only tests and quizzes? However, if teachers use this type of assessment, they need to be careful about consistency and fairness. This can be achieved with the use of rubrics because "they include criteria for a performance, descriptors of those criteria, and a scheme to arrive at a score" (PLAKANS and GEBRIL, 2015, p. 42).

There are three general types of scoring rubrics or scales: holistic, analytic, and primary trait. A holistic scale considers the test-takers' performance in a general way. It may contain descriptions for different features, but they are not considered separately. "The score represents an overall general level for the performance" (PLAKANS and GEBRIL, 2015, p. 44). Holistic scales are used mostly in high-stakes proficiency exams in which high levels of reliability need to be assured, so the performance levels are limited to usually four or five at the most. Raters should be extensively trained so that they can all judge the same piece of writing the same way. This guarantees consistency in scoring. The levels of performance typically represent the different proficiency levels.

Below is an example of the highest level on the TOEFL iBT independent writing task (Educational Testing Service):

An essay at this level largely accomplishes all of the following:

» Effectively addresses the topic and task
» Is well organized and well developed, using clearly appropriate explanations, exemplifications and/or details
» Displays unity, progression and coherence
» Displays consistent facility in the use of language, demonstrating syntactic variety, appropriate word choice and idiomaticity, though it may have minor lexical or grammatical errors

Holistic scales are not designed to offer correction, feedback, or diagnosis, so they lack educational potential. This is why the type of scale mostly used for classroom assessment of writing is the analytic one.

An analytic scale divides performance into various aspects and gives a separate score for each aspect. The separate scores can be added to obtain a general score. For example, considering the TOEFL descriptors above, if each descriptor received a separate score, ranging from 1 to 5, the total possible score would be 20, with distinct levels of performance ranging in between. A student could obtain a 5 in organization, but not necessarily in use of language, for example. Rather than ranging from 0 to 5, the scores would range from 0 to 20. This provides more feedback to students regarding the areas in which they performed well and the ones in which they were not so successful. However, it is still more of a scale than a rubric. To provide more detailed feedback to students, it is important to describe what each level of performance within each criterion is.

The third type of scale is the primary trait one, in which a checklist approach is used to determine if the performance has the desired features, and raters identify evidence for each of them, as exemplified by Plakans and Gebril (2015, p. 45):

1	Clear thesis statement.	YES	NO
2	Logical organization.	YES	NO
3	Introduction to engage reader.	YES	NO
4	At least two main ideas in the body.	YES	NO
5	Appropriate support for main idea.	YES	NO
6	Grammatical accuracy at least 90%.	YES	NO
7	Vocabulary used correctly at least 85%.	YES	NO
8	Sentence structures are varied.	YES	NO

If a final score is needed, points can be assigned to each category. These points do not need to be necessarily the same, but rather, they can reflect how important each trait is.

Table 7.1 shows an example of a checklist used to grade student performance on a specific writing task at the intermediate level.

Table 7.1 – Checklist for intermediate-level writing

CONTENT AND ORGANIZATION (10 PTS.)	YES	NO
The writer uses the given topic sentence and develops it clearly throughout the paragraph.	2	0
The paragraph has enough details that help maintain the reader's interest.	2	0
The paragraph has a concluding sentence that closes the text.	2	0
The paragraph presents the information in a logical order.	2	0
All information in the paragraph is about the topic.	2	0

GRAMMAR (4 PTS.)	YES	NO
There is no more than one mistake in verb tense and verb form.	1	0
There is no more than one mistake in articles and prepositions.	1	0
There is no more than one mistake in word order.	1	0
There is no more than one mistake in other language areas.	1	0

VOCABULARY (4 PTS.)	YES	NO
The writer uses appropriate vocabulary about parties.	1	0
The writer uses appropriate adjectives to describe parties and other events.	1	0
The writer uses words and phrases to link ideas.	1	0
There is no more than one mistake in word choice and word form.	1	0

MECHANICS (2 PTS.)	YES	NO
There is no more than one mistake in punctuation.	1	0
There is no more than one mistake in spelling and capitalization.	1	0

Examples of analytic scales

The most common type of rubric used for assessment of student achievement, rather than proficiency, is the analytic one because of its pedagogical advantage, as it provides detailed feedback on student performance that can inform students' future writing efforts. When analytic scoring rubrics became popular in the 80's, the scale commonly used was Jacob et. al's (1981, p. 30) ESL Composition Profile. The Profile is divided into five major writing components: content, organization, vocabulary, language use, and mechanics. Each component has four rating levels of "very poor", "poor to fair", "average to good", and "very good to excellent". Also, each component and level has clear descriptors of the writing proficiency for that particular level and a numerical scale. For instance, "very good to excellent" content has a minimum rating of 27 and a maximum of 30, indicating essay writing which is substantive, with thorough development of thesis, and relevant to the assigned topic. On the other hand, "very poor content" has a minimum of 13 and a maximum of 16 and indicates essay writing which does not show knowledge of the subject and is non-substantive and not pertinent. The maximum points for each rating category are: content, 30; organization, 20; vocabulary, 20; language use, 25; mechanics, 5. Hence, the categories do not receive the same weight in the assessment, as content and language use are regarded as more important than mechanics and vocabulary, for example.

Teachers from all over the world have adopted and adapted Jacob et al.'s (1981) rubrics, certainly assigning different points for the traits most valued in their context. As the use of scoring rubrics to assess student writing became widespread, curriculum developers and teachers also began developing their own rubrics to fit their contextual characteristics, such as student age, proficiency level, and curriculum focus.

Table 7.2 shows the scoring rubrics used for the assignment exemplified in Chapter 3, in which pre-intermediate students are asked to produce a proposal to ask for help or donations for a charity. It addresses the aspects that were focused on in the genre analysis and pre-writing stages. In other words, it is made clear to students what they have to include in their writing and they are eventually assessed based on these same premises. Rather than using a general rubric, a rubric designed especially for the task is used, focusing on the specificities of the assignment.

Table 7.2 – Rubrics to assess proposal for charity

CONTENT AND ORGANIZATION (12 PTS.)			
	YES	PARTIALLY	NO
The first paragraph specifies the problem.	3	2 - 1	0
The second paragraph explains how the problem affects the neighborhood or school.	3	2 - 1	0
The third paragraph suggests possible solutions.	3	2 - 1	0
Uses appropriate letter format.	3	2 - 1	0

GRAMMAR (12 PTS.)				
	YES	MOSTLY	PARTIALLY	NO
Uses verb tenses correctly.	4	3 - 2	1	0
Uses correct subject-verb agreement.	4	3 - 2	1	0
Uses appropriate sentence construction.	4	3 - 2	1	0

VOCABULARY (12 PTS.)				
	YES	MOSTLY	PARTIALLY	NO
Uses transition words to connect ideas.	4	3 - 2	1	0
Uses correct word form.	4	3 - 2	1	0
Contains little evidence of native language interference.	4	3 - 2	1	0

MECHANICS (4 PTS.)			
	YES	PARTIALLY	NO
Uses standard spelling and capitalization.	2	1	0
Uses standard punctuation.	2	1	0

Table 7.3 shows the rubrics used to assess the poster, activity also described in Chapter 3.

Table 7.3 – Rubrics to assess poster

CONTENT AND ORGANIZATION (12 PTS.)				
	YES	MOSTLY	PARTIALLY	NO
Contains an introductory sentence.	3	2	1	0
Includes the procedures that will guide the activities in the club.	3	2	1	0
Includes the place where the meetings will take place.	3	2	1	0
The design and layout are clear/creative.	3	2	1	0

GRAMMAR (12 PTS.)				
	YES	MOSTLY	PARTIALLY	NO
Uses verb tenses and forms correctly (especially present perfect).	4	3 - 2	1	0
Uses ever, before and never correctly.	4	3 - 2	1	0
Uses appropriate sentence construction.	4	3 - 2	1	0

VOCABULARY (12 PTS.)				
	YES	MOSTLY	PARTIALLY	NO
Contains little evidence of native language interference.	4	3 - 2	1	0
Uses correct word form.	4	3 - 2	1	0
Uses transition words correctly.	4	3 - 2	1	0

MECHANICS (4 PTS.)			
	YES	PARTIALLY	NO
Uses standard spelling and capitalization.	2	1	0
Uses standard punctuation.	2	1	0

Tables 7.4 and 7.5 show examples of rubrics that have been designed for specific writing assignments in a large ELT institute in Brazil. The rubrics on Table 7.4 are for a paragraph at a very basic level, following a model. The ones shown on Table 7.5 are for an assignment at the advanced level. In this case, because students write a draft and then a final product, they are assessed in these two stages. This resolves the practical aspect of some students never turning in their revised writing. They receive a grade on the piece they turned in, even if they did not rewrite it. Students who rewrite their texts have the chance not only to learn more but also to improve their grades. This system shifts the responsibility from the teacher to the student, as it is in his/her best interest to rewrite the piece. Students are also assessed with respect to their progress in the assignment.

Table 7.4 – Rubrics used for basic-level writing

Content:
4 - The paragraph addresses all the information stated in the model.
3 - The paragraph addresses some of the information stated in the model.
2 - The paragraph addresses a little information stated in the model.
Language use:
4 - Correct use of verb "to be", and articles.
3 - Two or three mistakes in the items described above.
2 - More than three mistakes in the items described above.
Vocabulary:
4 - Correct use of the vocabulary related to personal information.
3 - Two or three mistakes in the target vocabulary
2 - More than three mistakes in the target vocabulary.
Mechanics:
4 - Correct spelling, punctuation and capitalization.
3 - Two or three mistakes in spelling, punctuation and capitalization.
2 - More than three mistakes in spelling, punctuation and capitalization.

Table 7.5 – Rubrics for advanced-level writing

1st	2nd	CONTENT
22	22	The report is rich in relevant details, giving the reader a clear idea of the two classes. It successfully evaluates them and presents a solution to the problem.
18	18	The report has some relevant details, giving the reader a clear idea of the two classes. It fairly evaluates them and presents a solution to the problem.
14	14	The review could have more details. It partially gives the reader a clear idea of the two classes and does not present a logical solution to the problem.
6	6	The report doesn't have enough information to make the classes clear for the reader. It doesn't logically evaluate them or present a solution to the problem.
1st	2nd	ORGANIZATION
22	22	The introduction, body, and conclusion are effectively structured and connected.
18	18	The report is logically sequenced, but the introduction, body or conclusion is incomplete or unclear.
14	14	The report is not very logical because more than one of the three parts mentioned above is incomplete or unclear.
6	6	The report is not logical because it doesn't have the necessary components mentioned above.
1st	2nd	LANGUAGE STRUCTURE
20	20	There are only one or two errors in sentence structure which do not obscure communication.
16	16	There are some errors in sentence structure, but they do not obscure communication.
12	12	There are some errors in sentence structure, and a few may obscure communication.
6	6	There are many errors in sentence structure which obscure communication.
1st	2nd	VOCABULARY
16	16	Word choice is effective, with correct and appropriate word form. The writer uses words that express result and expressions with "take".
12	12	Word choice is effective most of the time, with a few problems in word form. The writer uses words that express result and expressions with "take".
8	8	Word choice is effective some of the time, with some problems in word choice and/or word form. The writer mostly uses simple vocabulary, with incorrect use of words that express result and expressions with "take".

▶

4	4	The vocabulary used is simplistic, with many problems in word choice and/or word form. The writer mostly uses very simple vocabulary, with no attempts at using words that express result and expressions with "take".
1st	2nd	MECHANICS
10	10	There are no errors in spelling, punctuation, capitalization, and/or paragraphing.
8	8	There are very few errors in spelling, punctuation, capitalization, and/or paragraphing.
6	6	There are some errors in spelling, punctuation, capitalization, and/or paragraphing.
2	2	There are many errors in spelling, punctuation, capitalization, and/or paragraphing.
1st	2nd	PROGRESS FROM 1ST DRAFT TO 2ND DRAFT
	10	Teacher's suggestions were effectively followed and the mistakes were effectively revised.
	7	Teacher's suggestions were mostly followed and the mistakes were mostly revised.
	5	Teacher's suggestions were partly followed and the mistakes were partly revised.
	0	Teacher's suggestions were not followed and the indicated mistakes were not corrected.

TOTAL		Comments:
1st draft	2nd draft	
____/90	____/100	

Portfolio assessment

Engaging students in all the stages of the writing process focused on in this book and assessing their final product by way of specific, well-developed scoring rubrics that will provide useful feedback is already an ambitious, albeit feasible and desirable goal in EFL integrated-skills classrooms. However, those who wish to go one step further in the formative assessment continuum should consider also adopting a portfolio assessment system.

The classical definition of portfolio is:

A portfolio is a purposeful collection of student work that exhibits the student's efforts, progress, and achievements in one or more areas. The collection must include student participation in selecting contents, the criteria for selection, the criteria for judging merit, and evidence of student self-reflection (PAULSON et al., 1991, p. 60).

Portfolios are not merely folders where students place all their assignments. The main components of portfolio assessment are student choice, engagement in self-reflection, and evidence of growth (PAULSON et al., 1991). Effective portfolio assessment will take into consideration the following aspects (HERMAN et al., 1996, p. 29):

» What is the assessment purpose?
» What tasks should be included in the portfolio collection?
» What standards and criteria will be applied?
» How will consistency in scoring or judgment be assured?
» Are the results valid for the intended purpose?
» How are the results used?

One of the main benefits of portfolios is their impact on teaching. Research has shown that classes become more student-centered and teachers are more relaxed and informal with students, resulting in more risk-taking behavior from both students and teachers (VIECHNICKI et al., 1993). Portfolio assessment is a type of authentic assessment, which refers to assessment based on information accumulated to indicate growth, gathered with variety of instruments, and usually teacher-constructed (STRICKLAND and STRICKLAND, 1998).

Below is a practical, realistic scheme for using portfolio assessment of writing in a skills-integrated EFL context:

1   Students engage in the number of writing tasks developed for the course, e.g. three, and the teacher follows all the stages suggested here, from

analyzing the genre to giving feedback, but without the need for formal rubrics or a score, perhaps just a checklist.

2. Students do not write the final product of each piece. They keep the drafts in a folder for future work. Depending on students' ages, these folders might be kept in the classroom so they do not get lost.
3. At the end of the period, students revisit their three pieces and choose two that they think more clearly demonstrate their writing ability and write a final product of these two pieces for their portfolio. In their rewriting of the selected pieces, students will use the knowledge they have acquired throughout the whole course and in the writing of the other assignments, and will have a chance to perform at their best.
4. Students write a cover letter explaining why they chose those two pieces and how the pieces demonstrate both their writing ability and their progress during the course.
5. Students put together their portfolio, including the cover letter and all the drafts of the two pieces they chose. If worksheets were used for generating ideas and planning, these can be included as well.
6. Teachers use scoring rubrics that address students' performance in the two pieces of writing and their growth over time, a very important component of portfolio assessment. Students receive a grade for their overall performance, and not on individual pieces.

An effective assessment system is one that uses multiple measures of student performance, so the portfolio grade can be averaged out with the other grades assigned during the course, such as written and oral tests and student participation.

Table 7.6 shows a scoring rubric that was used to assess the portfolio of advanced students in a writing course. It encompasses students' performance in the writing tasks and their participation in the complete process of drafting and revising. In the summative-formative continuum, this type of assessment can be categorized at the extreme end of a formative system, for it takes into consideration both the final product and students' participation in the process.

Assessing student writing

Table 7.6 – Portfolio rating rubrics

CONTENT	16	Substantive discussion of topics; support is consistent with thesis statements and is effective. Writing fully meets audience's needs.
	14	Clear discussion of topics. Support is mostly effective and substantive. Writing generally meets audience's needs.
	10	Fair knowledge of the subjects discussed; thesis statements are not always clearly stated; support is fairly substantive. Writing does not always meet audience's needs.
	6	Ideas are confusing. Thesis statements and support are mostly ineffective.
COHERENCE	14	Ideas are organized in a coherent, logical way; there are no ideas that do not belong. Writing is fluent and succinct.
	12	Organization of ideas is mostly effective; sequencing is logical but sometimes incomplete; introductions or conclusions might not be effective.
	8	Writing is somewhat choppy and loosely organized; sequence logical but incomplete.
	6	Writing is not fluent and lacks logical sequencing and development; ideas are confusing or disconnected.
COHESION	10	Ideas are linked appropriately by means of subordination coordination, and discourse markers.
	8	Writer clearly attempts to use cohesive devices but may fail occasionally.
	6	There is limited use of cohesive devices.
	2	There is ineffective or non-existent use of cohesive devices.
GRAMMAR	16	Writer uses a variety of sentence types effectively. No errors in language use.
	14	There are very few mistakes, and when they occur, they involve complex constructions. There is good control of verb formation, agreement, and tenses.
	12	Writer uses effective but simple constructions; there are a few errors of negation, agreement, tense, number, word order/function, articles, pronouns, prepositions and/or fragments, run-ons, and deletions.

▶

GRAMMAR	8	Writer is unable to use compound or complex structures; writer uses only simple structures and still makes mistakes in verb tenses and agreement.	
VOCABULARY	14	Writer uses a sophisticated range of vocabulary and makes effective word choice; there are no errors in word form.	
	12	Writer attempts to use a sophisticated range of vocabulary and makes very few mistakes in word forms.	
	10	Writer uses vocabulary adequate to the topic and makes some errors in word choice and usage.	
	6	Writer uses only common vocabulary and makes almost no attempt to use colorful vocabulary; many mistakes in word forms.	
MECHANICS	10	No errors in spelling and punctuation.	
	8	Very few errors in spelling and punctuation.	
	6	Some errors of spelling and punctuation.	
	4	Frequent errors of spelling and punctuation.	
	2	Dominated by errors of spelling and punctuation.	
PROGRESS	\multicolumn{3}{l	}{Student demonstrates the ability to revise compositions effectively, taking into consideration the relevant suggestions; student demonstrates ability to correct mistakes pointed out by peers/teachers; student tries to incorporate suggestions given on previous pieces of writings. 10 Yes 6 Partly 0 No 8 Most of the times 4 Rarely}
PARTICIPATION	\multicolumn{3}{l	}{Student wrote all the assigned essays in a timely fashion, bringing them well prepared for the peer review sessions and participating in them effectively. Second drafts were also produced on time. 10 Yes 6 Partly 0 No 8 Most of the times 4 Rarely}

Portfolios can be paper-based or electronic. There are a variety of tools that can be used to create e-portfolios, including blogs, wikis, Nings, or even the learning management system the institution already adopts. Whichever the tool used, they must be used in a way that maintains their core purpose, which is to aid students in metacognition, reflection, and ownership of learning (DAVIS, 2015).

Timed compositions and compositions on tests

It is not uncommon for language programs to require that students produce a timed paragraph or essay in class for a grade. This practice is grounded on the belief that we teach writing to prepare students for standardized tests. While it is true that the standardized-test paragraph or essay is one of the genres we should include in our curriculum, it is by no means the only one. In a lesson focused on writing this genre, it does seem logical to include a summative, timed writing assignment for students to demonstrate what they have learned. It is assumed here that they have practiced writing this genre, in accordance with the steps outlined in this book. If, however, the timed writing assignment is the only assignment in this genre, without the learning stage, then the task is merely assessing writing but not teaching it. If there are only timed writing assignments in the course, with no focus on teaching writing beyond these assignments, then students are also not learning writing, but rather, merely being assessed on written product. Also, timed writing assignments only make sense for the standardized-test writing genre, since in most other authentic situations in life in which we have to produce a piece of writing, we are not usually given only 30 to 60 minutes to produce the text.

A focus only on assessing writing without really teaching it also occurs when students are asked to write paragraphs or essays on tests without having gone through the process of learning how to produce these pieces of writing, in the same genre, throughout the unit of study on which the test is based. Sometimes the writing assignment on the test is not aimed at assessing a full range of writing traits, but rather, only grammar and sometimes vocabulary. In this case, it is not really writing that is being assessed; it is the use of a particular grammar structure and/or list of words within discourse. If this is made clear in the scoring system, it is an authentic and valid way of assessing grammar and vocabulary. Conversely, if students already produce pieces of writing throughout the grading unit and are assessed by way of rubrics, also including paragraphs or essays for assessment of writing competence on the test seems redundant and only aimed at putting more stress than necessary on students in a testing situation.

    This chapter concludes the orientation on how to conduct each stage of the writing process in an integrated-skills EFL context. The next and concluding chapter will sum up what has been presented in this book and provide guidelines on how to choose and/or adapt course books so as to fulfill all the writing orientation premises defended here.

After your read

- Do you now feel capable of designing or adapting scoring rubrics or checklists for your context?
- Think about the writing component in the curriculum you teach. Does it favor both the teaching and the assessment of writing or is it only focused on assessing writing? Are there rubrics to assess writing? Are they general or are they customized for each assignment, according to the genre?
- Do you agree with the suggestion given here that writing should be taught and assessed separately from tests?

THE FEEDBACK ON THE FINAL PRODUCT NEEDS TO HAVE A DIFFERENT FOCUS

Chapter 8

Putting it all together: using the process-genre framework to adapt materials

As mentioned in Chapter 1, it is very difficult to find skills-integrated materials in the English Language Teaching market that contain a writing component with all the features addressed in this book. The reason for this is not that the authors are not cognizant of what effective writing instruction should entail. The most likely explanation for the simplistic assignments found in many course books is that, in most contexts, writing is still treated as secondary in the curriculum and will only be given due attention later, probably in a separate Advanced Writing course or one focused on exam preparation.

However, writing is as important a skill, even at beginning levels, as speaking, listening, and reading. To communicate effectively in a second language, students need to develop the ability to produce texts in a variety of genres. Writing is still the means through which students and professionals are selected for educational programs or employment, for example. It is also the means through which people communicate with the world by way of social media and blogs. Even in video logs, so popular now on channels such as YouTube, the presenters probably produce some sort of writing, at least a script, before recording videos that will become viral and make them famous. Hence, writing is as alive as ever and a critical component of 21st Century skills.

There is no ideal course book, as each specific context requires a set of selection criteria that range from very practical ones, such as whether the content fits the course length, to more philosophical ones, such as whether the approach to teaching matches the institution's and teachers' beliefs about what language learning and teaching should entail. Other important criteria for course book selection involve the topics addressed vis-à-vis the students' age and interests, the balance between receptive and productive skills, how grammar and vocabulary are taught, the quality of the images and audios, among others. Thus, compromises always need to be made in relation to which of these criteria to prioritize.

When it comes to the approach to teaching writing, in the ideal world, these are the elements that an effective course book would contain:

1. A focus on a variety of genres and not just the school genre – the paragraph (for basic levels) and the essay (for more advanced levels).

2. A model text or texts in the genre students will have to produce. For practical purposes, this model text can be one used first for the development of reading skills per se. Genre analysis works more effectively if students have more than one model so that they can identify common features across texts of the same genre. This can be resolved if the publisher includes a text of the same genre as a workbook exercise, for example.
3. Genre analysis activities, and not just reading comprehension ones, in which students identify the features of that specific genre, as exemplified in Chapter 3. These activities should address the social purpose, structure, and linguistic features of the text.
4. Explicit instruction of rhetorical features, such as cohesive devices, pronoun reference, sentence structures typical of the genre, among others.
5. A writing task to produce the same genre and that proposes an authentic situation, with a clear context.
6. Activities for generating ideas and planning. These activities should vary so that students experience different strategies.
7. Peer revision activities.
8. Specific rubrics to assess student production.

Grabe (2001, p. 20) corroborates these recommendations when he states:

> Much like reading, writing, as a literate ability, requires extensive practice, supporting social contexts, opportunities to reflect and receive appropriate feedback, assistance with tasks across a range of genres, motivational support and positive experiences, opportunities to interact over the writing produced, and abilities to adapt and adjust purposes for writing.

In an analysis of six international course books used in a large language program in Brazil, it was found that none of them contained all the features above. In other words, there is no ideal course book, especially when it comes to the writing instruction component. The features most lacking are genre analysis, generating ideas and planning, peer revision, and specific rubrics. In fact, specific rubrics are not provided in any of the course books and peer review in only one, but in a very unstructured manner. However, the course books were selected due to their many other qualities and because these are aspects that can be easily included in the curriculum if the teacher and/or course developer are attuned to the content covered in this book.

The most critical situation is when the course book does not focus on a variety of genres in its writing activities. In this case, a parallel writing curriculum might need to be developed, based on the number of writing assignments to be worked on and the genres selected by the course developers as relevant for the specific age and proficiency level. These genres need to match the content of the lessons in the course book. Complete writing worksheets should be developed to include all the elements listed above. For example, in a lesson related to food and/or going to restaurants, students can work on the genre "restaurant review", and the worksheet can start with an authentic or authentic-like restaurant review for genre analysis.

Another critical situation is when there is genre variety, but there is only a writing prompt, following the sequence of activities in the book, and it is not clearly linked to a reading which can serve as a model, for example. In this case, the teacher will also probably have to develop a writing worksheet to go with the lesson. If there is a reading in a genre considered relevant for students at the given age and proficiency level, this text can be used as the model for genre analysis in the worksheet, which can direct students to the reading on the specific book page. If there isn't, the course developer needs to select a model and develop a complete worksheet around it. In basic levels, this model might have to be created or adapted from authentic materials. If the model is too far above students' proficiency level, it does not serve its purpose and can overwhelm the learners.

The more effective writing instruction features the course book contains, the fewer activities the accompanying worksheet will need to include. For example, for one of the course books used in the program mentioned earlier, the only three features that had to be added were the genre analysis activities, based on a model already provided, the peer revision, and the assessment rubrics.

Below is a description of a sequence of activities in the workbook that accompanies a pre-intermediate course book for teens. The bold-faced

Putting it all together: using the process-genre framework to adapt materials

parts are the tasks that were added to the existing sequence of activities to encompass all the features of our framework:

1. Students read a text about shark tank cleaners and answer multiple-choice comprehension questions.
2. **Students then answer other worksheet questions that address what type of text it is, where it was published, who would be interested in reading it, how it starts by grabbing the reader's attention, and how it is structured into paragraphs. They also circle the vocabulary that describes the characteristics of professionals who are good at this job.**
3. Students read tips provided in the workbook about giving opinions and reasons. They learn how to use transition words and how to organize reasons in discourse.
4. Students are given a prompt that instructs them to choose a job they would like to do in the future and write an e-mail explaining why they think they are the best person for the job. **The teacher provides a clearer social context for the e-mail, saying that the school director has asked them to write about the jobs they would like to have so that the school can organize a job fair and choose the jobs to focus on in the fair.**
5. The workbook instructs students to tell a partner which job they want and why they chose it. **To help students generate ideas, they are asked to make a list of the jobs they have thought of pursuing and the characteristics they think they should have to perform these jobs. They share ideas with their partners to complete their list. They also make a list of words they can use in their writing, especially adjectives to describe professionals' qualities.**
6. Students bring their writing to class, exchange papers, and fill out a checklist about their peer's writing. The checklist addresses issues that were discussed during the pre-writing activities, such as the content of the text, how it is organized, the transition words used to give opinions and reasons, and the vocabulary used. The teacher reads the peers'

feedback and complements it, also underlining mistakes and using symbols to help students self-correct.
7. **Students rewrite their e-mails.**
8. **The teacher assesses the final product using the same criteria in the peer revision activity.**

Depending on the students' profile and the specific genres they will need to learn, even when the course book contains writing activities aligned with the principles proposed by this process-genre framework, it might be necessary to develop a separate writing curriculum to match these specific needs. Our process-genre framework clearly delineates what this curriculum should contain, and this book has provided examples of how to develop each type of activity and assessment tool. Appendixes A and B consist of two complete writing activities that were developed for course books that either did not contain a variety of genres in their writing curriculum or presented such limited writing activities that the developers considered it more productive to rewrite them altogether. The worksheets encompass all the stages addressed in this book.

The main suggestion here is to use worksheets to fill the gaps in the course books or to develop a whole innovative writing program altogether. However, this can only be done effectively if teachers and course designers are able to identify these gaps and fill them. To this end, these professionals need to be well-versed in what constitutes effective writing instruction. As Kasten (2010, p. 3) states:

> Teachers are responsible for designing a classroom curriculum that is based on sound theory and research. Instructors should not surrender that core duty to antiquated criteria [...]. Students deserve course content that is driven by principled decisions based on professional experience, observation, and research.

This book has provided teachers and course designers with the tools to make these principled decisions as well as to evaluate the course materials and identify what is lacking or flawed and to develop effective and varied activities to complement the core materials, encompassing all the elements listed above.

Appendix A

Writing assignment to accompany an intermediate-level (B1) course book
Developed by Angela Minella

A. Discussion – Answer the following questions with a partner.
» If you could study in another country, would you do it? Why (not)? Where would you go?
» What are some difficulties a foreign exchange student may face?
» Imagine someone is coming to live in Brazil as an international student. What would you tell this person?
» Would you like to host an international student? Why (not)?

B. Analyze the text – Read the e-mail message below and answer the questions that follow.

> Dear Gabi, (   )
>
> How is it going? Hope you are well. I can only imagine how excited you must be! I'm really glad you are coming to live with us for a while. I'm sure it will be super cool! (   )
>
> Let me tell you a bit about my city. New York, as you know, is a really exciting and lively city. There are people from every part of the world living here, so it's often called a "melting pot". There are tons of places to visit, but my favorite one is Central Park, where there is an awesome mini zoo. Another place I love is the Metropolitan Museum of Art, which is huge! Also, there's the Empire State Building, one of New York's most well-known skyscrapers, which gives you a nice view of the city.
>
> My family is really small. I live with my Dad, my Mom and my brother Ricky, who is 17 years old. He is a pain! And we have a big dog, Spiky, who loves messing around. We live in Queens and our apartment is kind of tiny, so you will be staying in my room with me. Isn't that awesome?
>
> Be prepared to experience the cultural shock foreigners face. For example, we are always on the run, so we eat while walking on the street, on the bus or subway, anywhere! Also, we, teens, do volunteer work even during vacation, which is tiring but rewarding. And although this might surprise you, we are much friendlier than most people around the world think we are! (   )
>
> That's all for now. If you have any questions, just ask. I can hardly wait to meet you! :) (   )
>
> Carrie (   )

109

1   Who wrote the e-mail?
    _____
    _____

2   Who will read it?
    _____
    _____

3   What's the writer's purpose?
    _____
    _____

4   In this e-mail there is information about… (Mark all that apply.)
    ( ) The writer's family and home   ( ) The writer's favorite places
    ( ) The writer's school   ( ) Cultural differences
    ( ) The writer's city   ( ) The writer's hobbies

C. E-mail organization - Below you will see the parts of a well-structured e-mail (They are not in the correct sequence)

1   Sender's name: the writer's name.
2   Recipient: the person who will receive the message.
3   Greeting: a salutation to the recipient.
4   Opening paragraph: the reason why the e-mail is being written; a reference to a present situation.
5   Closing sentence: the final words.
6   Body: the most important content in the message; it can be made of different paragraphs.
7   Subject line: the topic.

Now you: Match the parts of an e-mail to the message in part B.

Appendix A

D. Focus on language - Informal language in writing

1 Observe these two sentences. Which one is informal? How do you know? Discuss.

Formal x Informal Language

Formal language is more common when we write; informal language, on the other hand, is more common when we speak. However, there are times where writing can be very informal, for example, when we write postcards or letters to friends, e-mails, blog posts or text messages.

Informal language can be related to words, contractions, slang and even to whole sentences. Examples of informal words: cool, a bunch, a bit, etc. Examples of informal sentences: "*See you later*" (*I'll see you later*), "*Hope you like it*" (*I hope you like it*), *What's up?*, etc.

2 Find examples of words and sentences that you think are informal. The first one has been done for you.

Hope you are well. (There's no subject in this sentence; it makes this informal.)

E. Preparing to write

Complete the diagram below with some key words to help you get ideas for your writing. Then, draw lines to make connections between the ideas.

Your family	City (details)	Brazilian eating habit
Brazilian fun activity	Your favorite places	City (description)
A brazilian habit	Your home	

F. Writing assignment

You're going to write an e-mail to a foreign exchange student who is coming to live with your family for some time.

- Start with a greeting and an introductory sentence (reference to the current situation: he/she is coming to live with you.)
- The body is going to be divided into three paragraphs, as follows:
  - Paragraph 1: Information about your town/city and your favorite places;
  - Paragraph 2: Information about your family;
  - Paragraph 3: Information about the brazilian culture.
- Write a closing sentence.
- Use some informal words and phrases.
- Use the model e-mail as a reference.

G. Peer review checklist

Read your peer's text and complete the checklist below:

Your text contains...

( ) ...a well-structured e-mail, with all the necessary parts.
( ) ...a reference to the present situation (your family hosting an international student).
( ) ...information about your city/town, your family and home, and some cultural aspects of your country.
( ) ...informal words or phrases that suit the genre.

My impressions as a reader:

( ) I was able to get a good idea of the writer's feelings towards the exchange student.
( ) The e-mail will make the student feel welcome and interested in his/her future experience.

H. Scoring rubrics

1st draft	2nd draft	CONTENT
22	22	The writer is able to write an effective e-mail to a prospective international student, providing detailed information about his/her city or town, favorite places, family, and cultural differences.
18	18	The writer is mostly able to write an e-mail to a prospective international student, providing information about his/her city or town, favorite places, family, and cultural differences.
14	14	The writer is partially able to write an e-mail to a prospective international student because it lacks some of the information that should be provided.
6	6	The writer's e-mail doesn't have enough relevant information to make it clear OR it doesn't address to topic of the assignment.

1st draft	2nd draft	ORGANIZATION
22	22	The e-mail is logically sequenced, containing all necessary sections (greeting, body and closing). The body contains three paragraphs. The ideas are clearly connected.
18	18	The e-mail is logically sequenced, but it may lack one of the necessary sections (greeting, body and closing). The body contains three paragraphs.
14	14	The e-mail lacks some of the necessary sections (greeting, body and closing) OR the writer includes ideas that are not connected to the topic.
6	6	The e-mail is not logical because it doesn't have the necessary parts. The ideas are disconnected.

1st draft	2nd draft	LANGUAGE STRUCTURE
20	20	Sentence structures are used appropriately, and there are no errors in verb/form, word order and/or sentence structure.
16	16	There are very few errors in verb/form, word order and/or sentence structure, which is adequate for the genre and the level.
12	12	There are some errors in verb tense/form, word order and/or sentence structure, which is mostly simple, but with a few instances of more complex structures.
6	6	There are many errors in verb tense/form, word order and/or sentence structure OR there are few errors, but the e-mail consists of very simple structures.

1st draft	2nd draft	VOCABULARY
16	16	Vocabulary is used very effectively in the entire text, with correct and appropriate word choice and word form. The writer uses informal language
12	12	Vocabulary is used effectively most of the time, with a few problems in word choice and/or word form. The writer makes some attempts at using informal language.
8	8	The vocabulary used is effective some of the time, with some problems in word choice and/or word form. The writer mostly uses simple vocabulary, with very few attempts at using informal language.
4	4	The vocabulary used is simplistic, with many problems in word choice and/or word form.
1st draft	**2nd draft**	**MECHANICS**
10	10	There are no errors in spelling, punctuation, capitalization and/or paragraphing.
8	8	There are very few errors in spelling, punctuation, capitalization and/or paragraphing.
6	6	There are some errors in spelling, punctuation, capitalization and/or paragraphing.
2	2	There are many errors in spelling, punctuation, capitalization and/or paragraphing.
1st draft	**2nd draft**	**PROGRESS FROM 1st DRAFT TO 2nd DRAFT**
	10	Teacher's suggestions were effectively followed and the mistakes were effectively revised.
	7	Teacher's suggestions were mostly followed and the mistakes were mostly revised.
	5	Teacher's suggestions were partly followed and the mistakes were partly revised.
	0	Teacher's suggestions were not followed and the indicated mistakes were not corrected.

TOTAL		Comments:
1st draft ____/90	2nd draft ____/100	

Appendix B

Writing assignment to accompany an advanced-level (C1) course book

Developed by Ana Netto

A. Think and discuss 1:

As we have been discussing, robots have been used in many fields, such as medicine, industry, science, construction, agriculture, among others. Think of the things they can do and give one example for each idea. Then discuss with a partner.

Jobs that humans do today but robots will do in the future	Jobs that humans can't do today but robots can	Jobs robots can do better than humans

B. Look at and analyze a model:

Read a model essay written in response to the question below and discuss the questions that follow it.

> It is believed that robots can replace humans in some activities. What kinds of activities can or should robots do instead of humans? What kinds of activities can't or shouldn't they do? Give reasons and examples in your response.

    Technological progress has brought many benefits to society. Powerful computers and artificial intelligence are no longer considered a thing of science-fiction movies. Nowadays, we have the alternative of relying on robots to do many activities for us. That said, I believe that some of those tasks can and should be performed by robots, whereas other kinds of tasks should be performed by humans for a number of reasons.

115

There are a number of fields in which robots can and should be used **as opposed to** *human beings*. Some fields involve dangerous activities, tasks requiring extreme precision, tedious, repetitive work, and activities that require huge computing power. For instance, take heavy industry, where robots are already used **instead of** human beings. Not only can they do dangerous or unpleasant jobs, they are also more efficient. Another good example of where robots are a good alternative to humans is in space exploration. (...)

On the other hand, there are some fields where a robot, however smart, would **be no substitute for** *a human being*. One example of this is caring for people in hospitals. Although robots can now perform surgery, human caregivers **rather than** robots are best at satisfying the psychological needs of patients. In fact, most patients **would rather** be cared for by a human caregiver than a robot. (...)

In sum, we live in a time when technological advances have the power of making a big difference in our everyday tasks. We should take advantage of all that those advances can offer, including the use of robots to perform certain kinds of tasks. We must, nonetheless, keep in mind that there are some activities that are, and in my opinion, will always be better performed by human beings.

1   What is the real purpose of this text?

   _____
   _____

2   Who are the probable readers of the text?

   _____
   _____

3   Where would you read this kind of text?

   _____
   _____

4 Circle the type of essay the sample is and then decide which items are related to it.

This is an **expository / opinion / evaluative** essay because…

( ) it involves the writer's opinion.

( ) it tries to convince the reader to agree with the author.

( ) the writer's arguments are reasonable and objective.

( ) it shows a point and a counter point.

( ) the writer's judgement is based on fair criteria.

( ) it brings reasonable evidence for the writer's arguments.

( ) it's impersonal.

C. Focus on language:

1 Notice the *expressions* in **bold**. What is their function? What kind of relationship do they establish between ideas?

D. Think and discuss 2:

1 On the website Debate.org, you will find opinions in favor or against drones. To what extent do you agree with these statements? Chose five opinions and rank them, giving a 5 to the one you agree with the most and a 1 to the one you agree with the least.

Available at: http://www.debate.org/opinions/should-drones-be-banned-from-private-use.

2 Now compare your ideas with your partner. Give reasons for your choices.

E. Generating ideas:

Brainstorm: Think of **as many areas or activities as you can** in which drones are being used. For each situation you think of, decide whether drones are beneficial or detrimental to society and write it below. Don't be selective at this point. Just let your ideas flow freely, taking notes of words, phrases or full sentences that come to mind.

Areas / Activities drones can be BENEFICIAL to society (and some reasons)	Areas / Activities drones can be HARMFUL to society (and some reasons)

F. Video and discussion:

Watch the video shown on YouTube about how drones have been used worldwide and check out if your ideas are shown on this video.

https://www.youtube.com/watch?v=1LNnFmwxVVU

G. Outline:

Go over your ideas in the chart above. Select the ideas (examples and reasons) that you think will best illustrate your viewpoint. Decide on the order in which you want to present these ideas.

H. Writing assignment:

You are going to write a four-paragraph essay in response to the following essay question:

> Drones are being widely used today, and their use is quite controversial. In what areas of society do you think using drones is beneficial? In which areas can drones be harmful?
> Give reasons and examples in your response.

Use expressions for stating alternatives and preferences in your writing.

I. Peer revision:

THE ESSAY
( ) The writer's opinion is clearly stated in the thesis statement.
( ) There are two body paragraphs
( ) Each body paragraph discusses one aspect of the writer's view.
( ) All supporting details are logically connected with linking words effectively illustrating the writer's opinion.
( ) The essay has expressions to state alternatives and preferences.
( ) The conclusion is powerful and expands the topic.

MY FINAL IMPRESSIONS AS A READER
( ) The article sounded very logical; it brings persuasive arguments.
( ) The title and introduction motivated me to keep reading the article.
( ) The language is neither excessively formal nor informal.
( ) The article is effective and the writer's point is quite reasonable.

J. Scoring rubrics

	CONTENT
24	The writer's opinion is clear and well defended. There is a point and counter-point, with plenty of evidence, details and/or examples.
20	The writer's opinion is somewhat clear and well defended. There is both a point and counter-point, with some evidence, details and/or examples.
16	The writer's opinion is clear, but it is not well defended. The distinction between the point and counter-point is not precise and it lacks sufficient evidence, details and/or examples.
8	The essay doesn't have enough relevant information to make his/her point clear OR it doesn't address the topic of the assignment.
	ORGANIZATION
24	The introduction and body are effectively structured, containing a clear thesis, topic sentences and supporting details. The conclusion provides a summary of the main points made in the essay.

20	The essay is logically sequenced, but the introduction, body or conclusion is a little abrupt or unclear.
16	The essay is not very logical because more than one of the three parts mentioned above is abrupt or unclear.
8	The essay is not logical because it doesn't have the necessary components mentioned above.
	LANGUAGE STRUCTURE
22	The writer tries to use more sophisticated language structures and there are no errors in verb tense/form, word order and/or sentence structure.
18	There are very few errors in verb/form, word order and/or sentence structure, which is adequate for the genre and the level.
10	There are some errors in verb tense/form, word order and/or sentence structure, which is mostly simple, but with a few instances of more complex structures.
5	There are many errors in verb tense/form, word order and/or sentence structure OR there are few errors, but the paragraph consists of very simple structures.
	VOCABULARY
18	Vocabulary is used very effectively, with correct and appropriate word choice and word form. The writer successfully uses expressions to state alternatives and preferences.
14	Vocabulary is used effectively most of the time, with a few problems in word choice and/or form. The writer tries to use expressions to state alternatives and preferences, but isn't always successful.
10	The vocabulary used is effective some of the time, with some problems in word choice and/or form. There are only one or two attempts to use expressions to state alternatives and preferences.
4	The vocabulary used is simplistic, with many problems in word choice and/or form. No attempts were made to use expressions to state alternatives and preferences.
	MECHANICS
12	There are no errors in spelling, punctuation, capitalization and/or paragraphing.

8	There are very few errors in spelling, punctuation, capitalization and/or paragraphing.
4	There are some errors in spelling, punctuation, capitalization and/or paragraphing.
2	There are many errors in spelling, punctuation, capitalization and/or paragraphing.
Grade:	Comments:
_____/100	

References

ATKINSON, D. L2 writing in the post-process era: Introduction. *Journal of Second Language Writing*, v. 12, n. 1, p. 49-63, 2003.

BAZERMAN, C. Speech Acts, Genres, and Activity Systems: How Texts Organize Activity and People. In: BAZERMAN, C.; PRIOR, P. (Orgs.). *What Writing Does and How It Does It: Introduction to Analysing Texts and Textual Practices*. Mahwah, NJ: Lawrence Erlbaum Associates, 2004, p. 309-340.

BELCHER, D.; HIRVELA, A. Introduction. In: BELCHER, D.; HIRVELA, A; (Orgs.). *Linking literacies: Perspectives on L2 reading-writing connections*. Ann Arbor: University of Michigan Press, 2001, p. 1-14.

BIBER, D.; GRAY, B.; POONPON, K. Should We Use Characteristics of Conversation to Measure Grammatical Complexity in L2 Writing Development?. *Tesol Quarterly*, v. 45, n. 1, p. 5-35, 2011.

BOSCOLO, P. Writing in primary school. In: BAZERMAN, C. (Org.). *Handbook of research on writing – history, society, school, individual, text*. New York: Lawrence Erlbaum Associates, 2008, p. 293-309.

BROWN, H. D. *Teaching by Principles - An Interactive Approach to Language Pedagogy*. White Plains, NY: Pearson Education, 1994.

CANAGARAJAH, A. S. *Critical academic writing and multilingual students*. Ann Arbor: The University of Michigan Press, 2002.

DAVIS, V. 11 Essentials for excellent e-portfolios. Edutopia, 2015. Available at "https://www.edutopia.org/blog/11-essentials-for-excellent-eportfolios-vicki-davis" https://www.edutopia.org/blog/11-essentials-for-excellent-eportfolios-vicki-davis. Retrieved on June 27, 2017.

DE OLIVEIRA, L. C.; LAN, S. W. Writing science in an upper elementary classroom: A genre-based approach to teaching English language learners. *Journal of Second Language Writing*, v. 25, p. 23-39, 2014.

EDUCATIONAL Testing Services. TOEFL iBT Scores. Available at https://www.ets.org/toefl/ibt/scores/understand/. Retrieved on June 22, 2017

FERRIS, D. *Treatment of error*. Ann Arbor: The University of Michigan Press, 2002.

FERRIS, D.; HEDGCOCK, J. *Teaching ESL Composition: Purpose, process, and practice*, 2nd ed. Mahwah, NJ: Erlbaum, 2005.

GRABE, W.; KAPLAN, R. *Theory and practice of writing*. London: Longman, 1996.

GRABE, W. Reading-Writing Relations: Theoretical Perspectives and Instructional Practices. In: BELCHER, D.; HIRVELA, A. (Eds.). *Linking literacies: Perspectives on L2 reading-writing connections*. Ann Arbor: University of Michigan Press, 2001, p. 15-47.

HARMER, J. *How to Teach Writing*. Essex, England: Pearson, 2004.

HERMAN, J. L.; GEARHART, M.; ASCHBACHER, P. R. Portfolios for classroom assessment: design and implementation issues. In: CALFEE, R. C.; PERFUMO, P. (Orgs). Writing Portfolios in the Classroom: policy, practice, promise, and peril. Mahwah, NJ: Lawrence Erlbaum Associates, 1996, p. 27-62.

HYLAND, K. *Second Language Writing*. New York, NY: Cambridge University Press, 2003.

HYLAND, K. Genre pedagogy: Language, literacy and L2 writing instruction. *Journal of Second Language Writing*, v. 16, p. 148-164, 2007.

JACOBS, H. L.; ZINGRAF, S. A.; WORMUTH, D. R.; HARTFIEL, V. F.; HUGHEY, J. B. *Testing ESL composition; A practical approach*. Rowley, MA: Newbury House, 1981.

JOHNS, A. M. L1 composition theories: implications for developing theories of L2 composition. In: KROLL, B. (Org). *Second language writing: research insights for the classroom*. New York, NY: Cambridge University Press, 1990, p. 24-36.

KASTEN, S. *Effective Second Language Writing*. Alexandria, VA: Teachers of English to Speakers of Other Languages, Inc., 2010.

KRATHWOHL, D. A revision of Bloom's taxonomy: An overview. *Theory Into Practice*, v. 41, n. 4, p. 212-218, 2002.

KROLL, B. Teaching writing in the ESL context. In: CELCE-MURCIA, M. (Org). *Teaching English as a second or foreign language*. New York: Newbury House, 1991, p. 245-263.

LIU, J.; HANSEN, J. G. *Peer response in second language writing classrooms*. Ann Arbor: Michigan University Press, 2002.

MATSUDA, P. K.; COX, M.; JORDAN, J; ORTMEIER-HOOPER, C. (2006). *Second language writing in the composition classroom – A critical sourcebook*. Boston: Bedford / St. Martin's, 2006.

MENASCHE, L. Silent Brainstorming. In: MUSSMAN, D. C. (Org.). *New Ways in Teaching Writing*. Alexandria, VA: Tesol International Association, 2013, p. 14-15.

MILLAR, D. Promoting Genre Awareness in the EFL Classroom. *English Teaching Forum*, v. 2, p. 2-15, 2011.

NATION, I. S. P. *Teaching ESL/EFL Reading and Writing*. New York: Routledge, 2009.

NEGHAVATI, A. Tools to help you give feedback in the digital world [web log]. *Teaching English*, August, 2016. Available at https://www.teachingenglish.org.uk/blogs/amin-neghavati/digital-tools-giving-feedback. Retrieved on April 29, 2017.

PAULSON, F. L.; PAULSON, P. R.; MEYER, C.A. What makes a portfolio a portfolio?. *Educational Leadership*, v. 48, n. 5, p. 60-63, 1985.

PLAKANS, L.; GEBRIL, A. *Assessment Myths – Applying Second Language Research to Classroom Teaching*. Ann Arbor: University of Michigan Press, 2015.

RAIMES, A. Out of the woods: emerging traditions in the teaching of writing. *TESOL Quarterly*, v. 28, p. 273-292, 1991.

REID, J. Writing. In: CARTER, R.; NUNAN, D. (Orgs.). *The Cambridge guide to teaching English to speakers of other languages*. Cambridge: Cambridge University Press, 2001, p. 28-33.

SILVA, T. Second language composition instruction: developments, issues, and directions in ESL. In: KROLL, B. (Org). *Second language writing: research insights for the classroom*. New York, NY: Cambridge University Press, 1990, p. 24-36.

STRICKLAND, K.; STRICKLAND, J. *Reflections on assessment: Its purpose, methods, and effects on learning*. Portsmouth, NH: Boyonton/Cook, 1998.

TSUI, A. B. M.; NG, M. Do secondary L2 writers benefit from peer comments?. *Journal of Second Language Writing*, v. 9, n. 2, 2000, p. 147-170.

VIECHNICKI, K.; BARBOUR, N.; SHAKLEE, B.; ROHRER, J.; AMBROSE, R. The impact of portfolio assessment on teacher classroom activities. *Journal of Teacher Education*, v. 44, n. 5, p. 371-377, 1993.

VYGOTSKY, L. S. *Thought and language*. London: Longman, 1986.

WEST VIRGINIA DEPARTMENT OF EDUCATION. *Graphic Organizers*. Available at https://wvde.state.wv.us/strategybank/GraphicOrganizersforWriting.html. Retrieved on June 22, 2017.

ZAMEL, V. The composing processes of advanced ESL students: Six case studies. *TESOL Quarterly*, v. 16, p. 195-209, 1983.

Este livro foi impresso na
LIS GRÁFICA E EDITORA LTDA.
Rua Felício Antônio Alves, 370 – Bonsucesso
CEP 07175-450 – Guarulhos – SP
Fone: (11) 3382-0777 – Fax: (11) 3382-0778
lisgrafica@lisgrafica.com.br – www.lisgrafica.com.br